MQ Publications Limited
12 The Ivories, 6–8 Northampton Street
London N1 2HY
Tel: +44 (0) 20 7359 2244
Fax: +44 (0) 20 7359 1616
email: mail@mqpublications.com

North American office
49 West 24th Street
New York, NY 10010
email: information@mqpublicationsus.com

website: www.mqpublications.com

ISBN: 1-84601-054-3

1 3 5 7 9 0 8 6 4 2

Printed and bound in China.

The Good JEWISH Home

Emily Haft Bloom

Illustrations by JayJay Studios

MQP

Acknowledgments

Though I am a Reform Jew, over the years I have learned a great deal about the intricacies of my faith. I attended Hebrew and religious school from age five to sixteen at a Reform synagogue and now dutifully drive my children to their religious training three times a week, between music lessons, sports, and my work as a writer. Though my faith doesn't define me exclusively, it does influence many aspects of my life. I try each day to instill in my children the same respect for their "Jewishness"; hopefully, they will allow it to be an integral part of their lives as well. I want to thank my knowledgeable and talented editor Sandy Gilbert, who continues to work diligently and patiently with me on book projects. She is a never-ending source of humor, wit, and serial commas.

I could not write one word without a terrific family backing me up. I want to thank my husband Don, who can always be counted on for encouragement and support and has finally learned to stay off my computer. My boys, Charlie and Timmy, are remarkably tolerant when waiting for their dinner or a ride to a game while I finish up a paragraph or two, and have also learned to stay off my computer. My dog, Rippy, known for her great appetite for leftover brisket and soggy matzoh balls, wraps herself around my chair while I write each day, risking great injury each time I get up. And of course, I must thank my mother and father, Marilyn and Herb Haft, who, together, provide the best example of the true meaning of *bashert*.

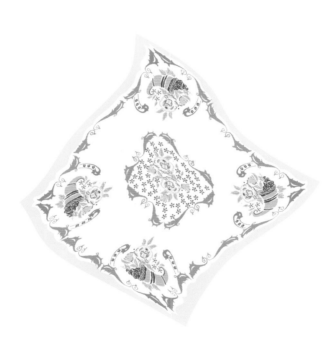

Contents

Introduction

Judaism is so much more than a religion. For the observant, it is a way of life steeped in tradition. What food you eat and clothes you wear, the way in which you find a spouse, how you raise your children, and even how you bury your dead were determined thousands of years ago. While Jewish tradition extends well beyond how to say the blessings over the wine and *challah*, Jewish wisdom provides a wealth of knowledge on issues ranging from business conduct to handling the *machetunim* (in-laws).

Jewish law has very specific guidelines for marking important milestones and how to observe the holidays. Even such mundane tasks as washing before eating and arising in the morning are daily rituals meant to be performed in a certain way, each with its own set of prayers and actions. Perhaps a better description of a Jew than someone who observes Judaism should be one who follows a template for existence.

There is comfort in knowing that families with a unique bond have observed the celebration of life, death, and everything in between the same way for centuries. However, the true beauty of being a Jew is the freedom to choose how you wish to live your life. While a great deal of traditional Jewish observances may seem impractical in the modern world, they can be incorporated in everyday life with a little compromise. Judaism can be all-consuming and influence every aspect of existence, or it can be simply celebrating *Shabbat* (the Hebrew word for Sabbath) or breaking the glass at the conclusion of a wedding.

Offering thoughts and guidance for the Reform Jew, the interfaith couple, and those with an interest in the traditions and wisdom of Judaism, this resource also includes passages from great Jewish thinkers, leaders, and biblical texts. Perhaps some of these writings will lead to a better understanding of why Jews do what they do when celebrating certain holidays and milestones. Ideas for holiday observances, recipes for traditional dishes, and recommendations for how to incorporate Judaism into your life can provide a strong foundation for any family.

Origins of the Jewish Faith

The Jewish religion has existed in one form or another, arguably, for over 3,800 years. The word "Jew" is most likely derived from the name Judah, the son of Israel (the most well-known of the twelve original tribes). This name became the one by which the survivors of the collapse of the Northern Kingdom of Israel became known.

The faith was borne out of Abraham's commitment to one god. Worshipping multiple gods (or idolatry) had been the only form of religious observance at that time. Although Abraham's belief in one god was perceived as radical then, he attracted many followers.

The law of the children of Israel is written in the Torah, or the first five books of the Bible, and to this day remains a source of inspiration, guidance, and thought for Jews all over the world. Besides the Ten Commandments, there are an additional 613 *Mitzvot*, or commandments, that were revealed to Moses, son of Abraham, at Mt. Sinai. While some of these may seem quaint or out of sync with modern society, they are meant to provide a moral compass. In a time when there were no books to consult and no advisors other than rabbis, rules on subjects as far-ranging as marital relations, planting the fields, raising children, and treating the poor were set down. To give you an idea of the nature of these laws, following find the first forty *Mitzvot*.

* To know that God exists
* Not to entertain the idea that there is any god but the Eternal
* Not to blaspheme, the penalty for which is death
* To hallow God's name
* To know that God is One, a complete Unity
* To love God
* To imitate His good and upright ways
* To honor the old and the wise
* To learn Torah and to teach it
* That every person shall write a scroll of the Torah for himself
* To relieve a neighbor of his burden and help to unload his beast
* To assist in replacing the load upon a neighbor's beast
* Not to leave a beast, that has fallen down beneath its burden, unaided

* Not to afflict an orphan or a widow
* To read the *Sh'ma* in the morning and at night
* Not to prophesy falsely
* Not to profane God's name
* To recite grace after meals
* Not to lay down a stone for worship
* To love all human beings who are of the covenant
* Not to stand by idly when a human life is in danger
* Not to wrong any one in speech
* Not to carry tales
* To rebuke the sinner
* Not to cherish hate in one's heart
* Not to take revenge

* Not to bear a grudge
* Not to put any Jew to shame
* Not to add to the Commandments of the Torah, whether in the Written Law or in its interpretation received by tradition
* Not to take away from the commandments of the Torah
* Not to curse any other Israelite
* To fear Him reverently
* Not to put the word of God to the test
* To cleave to those who know Him
* To circumcise the male offspring
* To put *tzitzit* on the corners of clothing
* To bind *tefillin* on the head
* To bind *tefillin* on the arm
* To affix the *mezuzah* to the doorposts and gates of your house
* To pray to God

In the Beginning (Bereshit)

IN THE BEGINNING GOD CREATED
THE HEAVEN AND THE EARTH
AND THE EARTH WAS IN DISARRAY
AND DARKNESS UPON THE ABYSS
AND THE SPIRIT OF GOD HOVERED (REPEAT)
UPON THE WATER
AND GOD SAID
LET THERE BE LIGHT AND THERE WAS LIGHT
AND GOD SAW THAT THE LIGHT IS GOOD
AND GOD SEPARATED BETWEEN THE LIGHT
AND THE DARKNESS
AND THE SPIRIT OF GOD (REPEAT)
AND GOD CALLED
THE LIGHT DAY, AND THE DARKNESS CALLED NIGHT
AND THERE WAS EVENING AND THERE WAS MORNING
DAY ONE.
AND THE SPIRIT OF GOD (REPEAT)

There is None Like Our God
(Ein Kelohaynu)

THERE IS NONE LIKE OUR GOD,
THERE IS NONE LIKE OUR LORD,
THERE IS NONE LIKE OUR KING,
THERE IS NONE LIKE OUR SAVIOR.

•

WHO IS LIKE OUR GOD, WHO IS LIKE OUR LORD,
WHO IS LIKE OUR KING, WHO IS LIKE OUR SAVIOR?
LET US THANK OUR GOD, LET US THANK OUR LORD,
LET US THANK OUR KING, LET US THANK OUR SAVIOR.

•

BLESSED BE OUR GOD, BLESSED BE OUR LORD,
BLESSED BE OUR KING, BLESSED BE OUR SAVIOR.
THOU ART OUR GOD, THOU ART OUR LORD,
THOU ART OUR KING, THOU ART OUR SAVIOR.
THOU ART THE ONE BEFORE WHOM OUR FATHERS
OFFERED THE SPICE OFFERING.

Chapter One

THE JEWISH FAMILY, MARRIAGE, AND HOME

The modern Jewish family is the epicenter of the faith and bears little resemblance to the Jewish family of biblical times. Back then, family structure was based on a strict interpretation of the law. Marriage, childbearing, child-rearing, and even the management of in-laws were dictated by scripture. Jews believe that an intrinsically strong family—in religion, education, and social endeavors—will be sound and peaceful. If any of these components are missing, the family will be weak and vulnerable to loss and discontent. Several rules based on the varied roles each family member plays are necessary for a joyful home life. This is not to say that Judaism won't recognize nontraditional roles. As long as everyone is content and relationships with one another are fulfilling, then the commandment for a peaceful home has been achieved.

According to scripture, three requirements must be met to satisfy the Torah's Commandments: each family member must be valued for what he or she contributes; *Shalom Bayit* (a peaceful and harmonious relationship) must be allowed to develop; and a democracy of sorts must exist so everyone's feelings are considered. One way to meet this expectation is to share equally the responsibilities of running a home, parenting children, and even caring for elderly parents. In my home, my husband works in an office and must commute each day. I work from home and so bear the responsibility for things he couldn't possibly manage. A fine balance is difficult to strike, but as the Torah commands, mutual respect for one another and valuing each person's contribution to the family is essential for a harmonious life together.

> *One who loves his wife and theirs as he loves himself and honors her more than himself shall know peace in his tent.*
> THE TALMUD

The Family

*Blessing is found in a home only by
virtue of his wife and theirs.*

THE NIDDAH

Judaism has always placed a tremendous emphasis
on education and intellectual development. Parents
are expected to provide their children with the
training for both a livelihood as well as for
conducting their daily lives. A Jew needs to be
equipped to support a family, but he or she must also
be prepared to make wise decisions throughout life.
This knowledge should come not only from religious
study, but also from the secular world of music, art,
science, and literature.

Instilling moral values is considered equal to
intellectual education, and it should begin as soon as
a child is able to understand. The excuse that younger
children don't know right from wrong is not
acceptable to most observant Jews; children should
be taught to respect the Torah and its teachings and
the tenets of Jewish history as early as possible. Many
parents choose not to bring their children to
synagogue services until they are old enough to sit
still and keep quiet. Children's services are an
alternative to a longer adult service but can also be
devoid of the solemnity and piousness that certain

holidays require. I recall my first adult service as dreadfully long and drawn out but astonishingly quiet and calm after years of the free-for-all children's services I had always attended. Some children, particularly those raised in Orthodox homes, know no other service than that which lasts hours, requires silence and reverence; and tolerates no squirming and fidgeting.

Besides Torah study, Judaism offers innumerable other chances for families to honor its traditions. The celebration of the many festivals, holidays, and the Sabbath are meant to bring families together. My family tries to share a Friday night *Shabbat* dinner together when we can because we have made a commitment. The *Shabbat* candle lighting and blessings over the wine and *challah*, and attending synagogue as a family, is a great start to fulfilling the Torah's commandment that the Jewish home be one of peace, mutual respect, and love.

> *Train the child*
> *according to his way.*
> THE TALMUD

Marriage.

*First build a house, then plant a
vineyard, and after that, marry.*

THE BIBLE

Marriage is a sacred institution in every religion, but for Jews there is a lot more to finding the right partner and settling down. The Talmud says that forty days before a male child is conceived, a voice from heaven announces whose daughter he is going to marry. Perhaps this is the origin of the expression "a match made in heaven." Often when a good match has been made, those who know Yiddish will say it is *bashert*, meaning that it is good fortune and a soul mate or the right partner has been found. The concept of *bashert* is important, but the Talmud also advises men to seek a wife based on many other factors. These include from whom she is descended and the compatibility of the two families. Since the Talmud was written in a time when a man sought a wife, and women did not search for a partner themselves, it provides direction for men only.

Unlike some other religions, Judaism does not forbid divorce. Though it is never welcome, the biblical texts tell us that an unhappy marriage need not be kept intact and second marriages are acceptable. A woman may seek a divorce based on her dissatisfaction with her husband, his failure to meet her needs, or his unfaithfulness. The Talmud says that God has a hand in arranging these second chances too. Consistent with the belief that whole families need to be content in order to fulfill the commandments, unhappiness should be dealt with and not swept under the rug and hidden from the neighbors.

In the Orthodox faith, Jews follow the laws of courtship closely, and to this day a couple will not spend time alone together before they are wed. Arranged marriages do still take place, though mostly in ultrareligious communities. Many are arranged between a bride and groom from overseas and could be seen by some as mergers of sorts as prominent families expand their power and scope by joining together their sons and daughters. Even in less observant communities, and among Reform Jews, marrying within the faith is very important. Intermarriage, it is believed, dilutes the already small population of Jews and unless the non-Jewish spouse-to-be converts, can be complicated.

Jewish mothers have gotten a bad rap trying to marry off their children to their friends' children, but in truth it really makes a lot of sense to try and arrange a *shiddach* (arranged marriage). Sometimes, the effort is made under false pretenses; for example, "wouldn't you like to see my son's lovely new apartment" really means he's single and needs a hand in finding an appropriate wife. On any given weekend in cities with large Jewish populations, there are singles events thinly disguised as benefits for Jewish causes, gatherings at social clubs, and in early December of each year in New York City, the Matzoh Ball, a festive gathering of Jewish singles. Matchmaking isn't always successful, and there is no guarantee that if you attend enough of these sorts of parties that you will eventually walk out of one with your bashert, but it certainly increases the odds. I too tolerated my share of blind dates, dinner parties seated next to a conveniently single man, and benefits for Jewish causes, in search of the right guy and finally found him...at a gathering of Jewish singles at a private club.

But, sometimes, a mother's best intentions don't work out and a child will marry outside the faith. Intermarriage, once considered unthinkable for a Jew, has become so widespread that it is only the most observant Orthodox and some Conservatives that will find serious fault with it. Many non-Jews will continue to observe their own religions, and some will participate in both celebrations and holidays. Often the non-Jew will participate in a conversion program to introduce him or her to the Jewish faith, its history, and the basics of Jewish prayer and celebrations. Most Reform rabbis will marry an interfaith couple. Many Conservative and most Orthodox will not perform the service unless a complete conversion has taken place, including a *mikvah* (a ritual bath for the woman) and a ceremonial *bris* (circumcision for the man). Despite a remaining smidgen of sadness over an interfaith union, Judaism is, essentially, an inclusive religion, offering all a chance to participate and pray. Families not bound by marriage, single-parent homes, and gay and lesbian families all can and do participate fully in Jewish life.

How good and how pleasant it is for brethren to dwell together in unity.

PSALMS

A non-Jewish Roman woman asked a rabbi, "If your God created the universe in six days, then what has He been doing with his time since He finished?" The rabbi said that God has been arranging marriages. The Roman woman laughed and said that arranging marriages was a simple task, but the rabbi assured her that arranging marriages properly is as difficult as parting the Red Sea. To prove the rabbi wrong, the woman went home and took a thousand male slaves and a thousand female slaves and matched them up in marriages. The next day, the slaves appeared before her, many with horrid injuries and others just appearing miserable, and asked to be released from their marriages. The woman went back to the rabbi and said, "There is no god like your God, and your Torah is true."

UNKNOWN

Of the 613 *Mitzvot*, many pertain to proper conduct in a marriage. Some of these may seem painfully obvious or even ridiculous—not too many people need to consult their Torah to know they shouldn't commit incest or withhold food and clothing from their wives—but many have merit in contemporary society. Listed here are those that apply to the family and marriage:

* To honor father and mother

* Not to smite a father or a mother

* Not to curse a father or mother

* To reverently fear father and mother

* To be fruitful and multiply

* That there shall be no harlot (in Israel); that is, that there shall be no intercourse with a woman, without previous marriage with a deed of marriage and formal declaration of marriage

* To take a wife by *kiddushin*, the sacrament of marriage

* That the newly married husband shall (be free) for one year to rejoice with his wife

* That a bridegroom shall be exempt for a whole year from taking part in any public labor, such as military service, guarding the wall, and similar duties

* Not to withhold food, clothing, or conjugal rights from a wife
* That the woman suspected of adultery shall be dealt with as prescribed in the Torah
* That one who defames his wife's honor (by falsely accusing her of unchastity before marriage) must live with her all his lifetime
* That a man may not divorce his wife concerning whom he has published an evil report about her unchastity (before marriage)
* To divorce by a formal written document
* That one who divorced his wife shall not remarry her, if after the divorce she had been married to another man
* That a widow whose husband died childless must not be married to anyone but her deceased husband's brother
* Not to indulge in familiarities with relatives, such as kissing, embracing, winking, skipping, which may lead to incest
* Not to have intercourse with another man's wife

A man cannot live without a woman,
a woman cannot live without a man,
and the two of them cannot live without
the presence of God.

THE BIBLE

The family is a sacred element of Judaism and the Bible and great Jewish scholars have much to say on this topic:

Blessed art Thou, O Lord our God, King of the Universe, who created mirth and joy, bridegroom and bride, gladness, jubilation, dancing, and delight, love and brotherhood, peace and fellowship. Quickly, O Lord our God, may the sound of mirth and joy be heard in the streets of Judah and Jerusalem, the voice of bridegroom and bride, jubilant voices of bridegrooms from their canopies and youths from the feasts of song. Blessed art Thou, O Lord, who makes the bridegroom rejoice with the bride.

THE TALMUD

*He who has no wife is not a proper man,
without joy, blessing, goodness, Torah,
protection, and peace.*

THE BIBLE

•

*Therefore a man shall leave his father
and mother and cleave to his wife, and
they shall become one flesh.*

GENESIS

•

*A man must be exceedingly careful
to show honor to his wife.*

ANCIENT JEWISH TEXT

It was the custom in Ancient Egypt
that when a boy was born, a cedar tree
was planted and when a girl was born, a
pine tree was planted. When they grew
up and married, the chuppah (wedding
canopy) was made from branches taken
from both trees.

THE TALMUD

•

God spent the first six days making
Heaven and Earth and has been occupied
since with making matches. Jews believe
that only God can find one's true bashert
(one's fated or destined partner).

UNKNOWN

The Wedding

The celebration of a marriage in the Jewish faith is replete with ritual and tradition. Each step from the engagement to setting up the first home may follow the guidelines established in sacred texts and there are reasons for all of them. For example, Jewish law established that men and women have equal rights and women are not property to be owned. The couple to be married is not joined together by a member of the clergy; they marry each other with the clergy's assistance.

The marriage ceremony may be preceded by a few events including a visit to the *mikvah* and an *aufruf*. The *mikvah* (a ritual bath) prepares the bride-to-be by assuring her physical and spiritual cleanliness. It is a ritual founded in practicality. Stop and think how many women before you went to the *mikvah* before they were wed, and it will seem like a wonderful way to enter into the next part of your life as a Jewish woman. An *aufruf*, a German phrase for calling up, involves a Torah reading shared by the bride and groom before the ceremony and usually takes place on the Sabbath immediately preceding the wedding. It concludes with showering the couple with nuts or other sweets by friends and family.

More observant Jews assure that the wedding does not take place during the bride's menses because that would make it impossible to consummate the marriage on the wedding day since she is deemed unclean at that time. Many Jews prefer not to plan a wedding on a Jewish holiday or during *Shabbat* since, according to tradition, it is unwise to celebrate two *simchas* (joyous celebrations) at once.

> *It is better to live one's life with another than alone.*
> THE MISHNAH

•

> *A wifeless man exists without joy, without blessing, or boon.*
> THE MISHNAH

The Ketubah

During the wedding ceremony, there are several traditions that even the most Reform Jews include. The first is the signing of the *ketubah*, a Jewish marriage certificate. This marriage contract can be a magnificent hand-painted artwork or a simply written document. The *ketubah* is intended to assure the rights of both parties in the marriage. This marriage contract is signed by witnesses from both the bride and groom's sides. At many contemporary weddings, the bride and groom will spend a few minutes or more with the rabbi signing the document. Other family members may be present or the rabbi may wish to impart a few last words of wisdom before the walk down the aisle.

My husband and I chose a handwritten *ketubah* that contains many visual metaphors for marriage and Judaism. We have hung it in our bedroom at home as a constant reminder of our commitment to each other. When we first began to look for a home in which to move our growing family, I remember seeing several *ketubot* hanging in the same spot in prospective houses. One couple I know had their own *ketubah* created for them by a calligrapher and artist familiar with the required language. It is decorated with their Hebrew names and includes symbols of their lives together.

This is the day which the Lord hath
made; On it we will be glad and rejoice!

•

Let the bridegroom go forth from
his chamber and the bride out of
her pavilion.

THE BIBLE

•

Behold, thou art consecrated unto me.

TRADITIONAL JEWISH MARRIAGE SERVICE

•

Whenever a married man and woman
argue loudly and intensely, they should
stop and read together the words of their
ketubah to one another and it shall
serve as a reminder.

BA'AL SHEM TOV

Chuppah

The next tradition is marrying under the *chuppah* (a marriage canopy). The *chuppah* is symbolic of the creation of a new home and functions as a holy place for the ceremony. It can be as simple as a *tallit* (Jewish prayer shawl) draped over a frame or may be as elaborate as an intricately woven array of branches, flowers, or family heirlooms such as an antique *tallit* or a bridal veil. I attended one wedding at a Napa Valley vineyard at which the *chuppah* was composed of olive branches, grapevines, and almond branches interwoven with two grandfathers' *tallit*. It was symbolic of family, the fruits of Israel, and the bride and groom's chosen careers in winemaking.

Therefore must the bride have a canopy,
all beautiful with decorations prepared
for her to honor the Bride above,
who participates in the joy of the bride
below. This is why it is necessary
that the canopy be as lovely as
possible and the Supernal bride be
invited to share the joy.

ZOHAR

Breaking of the Glass

The last and most familiar of these traditions is the breaking of the glass. Usually, a wine glass is wrapped in a napkin and placed beside the groom's feet. At the conclusion of the service, the groom stomps on the glass until it breaks; often this requires more than one attempt. Some say this is a reference to the destruction of the temple in Jerusalem. Others think it acts as a talisman against evil spirits. Jewish scholars believe it stems from an episode in Jewish history when a rabbi was trying to get the wedding guests' attention when they became too raucous. Whatever its origins, the breaking of the glass has become an enduring symbol of the end of the marriage ceremony and the beginning of life together. Failing to break the glass on the first try is not considered bad luck nor is it a harbinger of evil; as a matter of fact, getting a grip on the first try on a slippery napkin wrapped around a cylindrical glass object at possibly the most nerve-wracking moment of a Jewish man's life is quite a feat.

Set me as a seal upon thine heart.

SONG OF SONGS

●

*O friends of the wedded pair, haste now
to drink the wine of friendship from
the bowl of joy.*

TRADITIONAL WEDDING PRAYER

●

*If a man and wife are worthy, the divine
presence is with them.*

THE TORAH

Wedding Bands

Some Jews observe other traditions at their wedding ceremonies. One popular example is the exchange of plain gold bands, without stones or other decoration. These simple wedding bands—perfectly smooth circles without bumps—are meant to symbolize a life together without ups and downs. A bride that prefers a more decorative band may choose to borrow a parent or sibling's unadorned ring for the ceremony and receive their own after the service.

I will betroth thee unto me in righteousness.

THE BIBLE

We now know that Jewish law carefully proscribes that there must be mutual respect between husband and wife and every aspect of the marriage must reflect that. Wives have the right to expect contentment, satisfaction, and affection as much as their spouses. They even have the right to sexual satisfaction and pleasure. As a recognized important aspect of any marriage, the Torah got it right when it made mutual pleasure a commandment.

> *Behold thou art consecrated unto me by this ring according to the law of Moses and Israel.*
>
> JEWISH WEDDING VOW

If a man forbids himself by vow from
having intercourse with his spouse for
more than two weeks, she may
divorce him.

THE MISHNAH

•

For most people there is nothing harder
in the entire Torah than to abstain from
sex and forbidden relations.

MAIMONIDES

•

Were it not for the evil inclination, no
man would build a home and marry.

THE BIBLE

•

Two are better than one, for if they fall,
one will lift the other up.
Woe to him who falls alone and has not
another to lift him up.
And, if two lie together,
they have warmth;
but how can one be warm alone?

ECCLESIASTES

The Home

*And you shall speak of them when
you sit in your house, when you walk by
the way, when you lie down, and when
you rise up. And you shall write them
upon the doorposts of your house and
upon your gates.*

SH'MA

The traditional Jewish home may include many examples of Judaica—art, sculpture, religious items, and books—but must have one in particular to be a true Jewish household—the *mezuzah* (Hebrew for doorpost). The *mezuzah* is a small case for a copy of the *Sh'ma*, a prayer that acknowledges belief in one God. The *Sh'ma* should be handwritten on parchment by a scribe. In some homes, the *mezuzah* is mounted on the frame of the front and back doors at about eye level, on the right side, tilted so the top is toward the door. Some choose to mount a *mezuzah* on each door frame in the home, particularly at the entrance to bedrooms.

All rooms, with the exception of bathrooms and closets, may have one. An appropriate housewarming or baby gift, the *mezuzah* can be any style—traditional, modern, or contemporary—as long as the sacred text is included. This is a popular item to purchase in Israel; one of mine was a gift from a friend who traveled to Israel and is decorated with Eilat, a stone turquoise in color and culled from what is said to be King Solomon's mines.

Whosoever has the tefillin on his head, the tefillin on his arm, the tzitzit on his garment, and the mezuzah on his doorpost, is fortified against sinning.

THE BIBLE

•

Hear, Israel, the Lord is our God, the Lord is One.

DEUTERONOMY

Jewish Literature

Each home should have a copy of the Torah, the Bible, and the Talmud, as well as other scholarly works and Jewish literature. Often these books are given by synagogues upon the occasion of a *Bar* or *Bat Mitzvah* or Confirmation and should be taken whenever the recipient moves into a new residence.

AL SH'LOSHA D'VARIM

Al sh'losha d'varim ha'olam omed;
Al hatora, v'al ha'avoda,
v'al g'milut chasadim

TRANSLATION:

The world stands on three things—On Torah, on worship, and on good deeds.

Menorah

The *menorah* is another symbolic piece of Judaica that many Jewish homes often display. Originally a candelabrum when oil was used as a source of light, it is now most frequently associated with Chanukah, the "Festival of Lights." The original *menorah* had space for seven dishes of oil. The Chanukah *menorah* (or *channukiah*) has eight and one more in the center. Again a *menorah* may be decorated in any style and is another traditional gift for a new home.

A miracle occurred when the menorah was kindled for eight days. These days were set aside for the rendering of praise and thanksgiving.

THE TALMUD

The Laws of Kashrut or a Kosher Home

The word kosher has entered the English vernacular and has come to mean acceptable, approved, or otherwise OK. What it really means is a great deal more. A kosher home is one that follows a strict set of rules for what is eaten, when it is served, and how it is prepared. It also means, as explained later, wearing clothing and even using cleaning products made from kosher animals. Keeping a truly kosher home is an enormous undertaking and requires a lifetime commitment, and a lot of extra cookware. But for many it is simply a part of life that becomes part of their devotion to the faith. If one is raised kosher, setting up a new home with a kosher kitchen seems a natural choice. For those who make the decision to keep kosher later in life, the desire to adhere to the rules will likely be more important to them than the inconvenience it will cause.

Many Jews will say that they keep kosher at home, but not when eating out. But to truly keep kosher means making the commitment full-time. Eating spare ribs at the Chinese restaurant on Sunday night is not a biblically acceptable exception, nor is having a cheeseburger even if you hold the bacon.

Kosher means buying your meat and poultry at a kosher butcher and never purchasing sliced turkey at the deli counter unless they maintain a separate slicer and case for the kosher meats.

It also means having four sets of dishes, cutlery, and pots and pans for your meat and dairy, and Passover meat and dairy. It may also mean two separate dishwashers and refrigerators. For the observant, buying your clothing from a shop that carries kosher clothing is also a requirement. In other words, it is a vast undertaking. But, for many Jews it is simply a part of their daily observance.

It is easy to understand where many of the laws of *Kashrut* came from. Some reinforce what is common sense, such as not eating fruit with worms or vermin, or animals that have died of disease. Others tend to be more arbitrary, but perhaps when they were written there was good reason to be wary. The 613 *Mitzvot* (or rules) proscribe exactly what can and cannot be eaten, how animals are meant to be slaughtered, and even which insects may be consumed. The following are the *Mitzvot* that pertain to the dietary laws:

* To examine the marks in cattle so as to distinguish the clean from the unclean

* Not to eat the flesh of unclean beasts

* To examine the marks in fishes so as to distinguish the clean from the unclean

* Not to eat unclean fish

* To examine the marks in fowl, so as to distinguish the clean from the unclean

* Not to eat unclean fowl

* To examine the marks in locusts, so as to distinguish the clean from the unclean

* Not to eat a worm found in fruit

* Not to eat of things that creep upon the earth

* Not to eat any vermin of the earth

* Not to eat things that swarm in the water

* Not to eat of winged insects

* Not to eat the flesh of a beast that is *terefah*

* Not to eat the flesh of a beast that died of itself

* To slay cattle, deer, and fowl according to the laws of *shechitah* if their flesh is to be eaten

* Not to eat a limb removed from a living beast

* Not to slaughter an animal and its young on the same day

* Not to boil meat with milk

* Not to take the mother-bird with the young

* To set the mother-bird free when taking the nest

* Not to eat the flesh of an ox that was condemned to be stoned

* Not to eat flesh with milk

* Not to eat of the thigh-vein which shrank

* Not to eat *chelev* (tallow-fat)

* Not to eat blood

* To cover the blood of undomesticated animals

* Not to eat or drink like a glutton or a drunkard (not to rebel against father or mother)

These rules are often confusing and there are many debates still to this day on the subject. For the very observant, garments and footwear must be made from kosher animals. Questions about the origins of their shoe leather, the wool for their coats, and the tallow for their soap makes the commitment to a kosher life extend far beyond the kitchen.

The following is a simplified guide to what is kosher:

* Animals that chew their cud are kosher; those that do not and those without cloven hooves are not. Materials from these animals, such as camel's hair and rabbit fur are strictly off limits.

* Animals that are technically kosher must be slaughtered according to specific rules. Certain parts of these animals are not kosher. Since no blood may be consumed, kosher animals need to be salted and soaked to remove any residual blood; plus the salting makes everything taste better!

* The greater expense incurred in raising and dressing kosher livestock is the reason for the higher price. Further inspection of slaughtered animals is required to determine that it is healthy

or *glatt* (smooth). *Glatt* is the highest kosher standard. Anything caught from the sea must have scales and fins, so shellfish is not considered kosher. The kosherness of fish like swordfish is debatable as their scales are subject to interpretation.

* Game birds such as quail, pheasant, and geese are not kosher.

* Certainly the most confusing aspect of *Kashrut* is the forbidden cooking of an animal in its mother's milk. This means that no meat may be served with dairy; no cheeseburgers, no steak with béarnaise made with cream, and no chicken Cordon Bleu. Cookware and dishes must be maintained to prepare both *milchig* (dairy) and *fleishig* (meat). A specific amount of time must elapse between a meat or dairy meal before consuming the other.

* *Parve* foods are neutral foods, and can be eaten with both milk and dairy. These include all fruits, vegetables, nuts, and grains.

Whatever the reasons for the evolution of these laws, kosher foods are usually prepared under strict supervision, and according to stringent health requirement. What could be wrong with that? For those that choose not to keep a kosher home and enjoy tucking into a cheeseburger right off the backyard grill, buying kosher beef can be a compromise, but it doesn't make you kosher. Kosher poultry routinely wins taste tests as the brining process makes it moister, more tender, and a whole lot tastier.

In Jewish history, a great deal of importance was attached to following the laws of *Kashrut*. In ancient times, Jews were often ridiculed, mocked, and bullied because of their eating habits. Oppressors often tortured Jews in an attempt to get them to eat forbidden foods; many chose to suffer rather than break the dietary laws. For some Jews, kosher has become a way of life, and never having tasted lobster or shrimp is a very small sacrifice in the observance of their faith.

Though my mother was raised in a kosher home, my father was not. His knowledge of *Kashrut* was so minimal that, before they were married, when he arrived to take my mother out on a date, he offered to help clear the dishes from the just completed meal and proceeded to place the dishes in the wrong sink. He recalls thinking to himself, "Good thing I won't be coming back here!". Despite this *Kashrut* faux-pas, they have remained happily married for more than forty-seven years. My mother, though no longer kosher, still prohibits mixing meat and dairy at holiday meals and I don't ever recall bacon, pork, or ham ever being prepared in an otherwise very busy kitchen. She does however enjoy the occasional order of spare ribs and relishes her summer lobster in Maine.

Thou shalt not seethe a kid in its mother's milk.

PENTATEUCH

•

Every creature that lives shall be yours to eat; you must not however eat flesh with its blood in it.

GENESIS

•

Eating swine's flesh and the detestable thing and the mouse, shall be consumed together.

THE BIBLE

•

Many of the people of Israel adhered to the law of the Lord. They would not eat unclean things, and chose rather to die.

MACCABEES

Chapter Two

THE JEWISH LIFE CYCLE

Milestones

There are many traditions and rituals associated with the milestones in a Jew's life and some are celebrated the same way they were observed over 3,800 years ago. Perhaps the reason for keeping these traditions alive for so long is that during the many periods of Jewish oppression, there were only a few things that Jews could be sure of—children would be born, people would get older, and they would die. While there may not have always been a synagogue to pray in, a Torah to read from, a festive table to set, and delicious food to eat, these events could always be observed, if only from memory. Therefore, Jewish families place great importance on marking the occasions of birth, *Bar* or *Bat Mitzvah*, marriage, and death with piety, reverence, and an eye on history.

According to Jewish law, the essential purpose of marriage is to procreate—it is a *mitzvah*. In fact, the Bible tells us to "be fertile and increase." The commandment to multiply is taken more seriously by those in the Orthodox and Hasidic communities. Men are prohibited from "spilling their seed", so condoms and vasectomies are not permitted. Marrying young, Orthodox women often have five children before they reach thirty and many don't stop there. The law says that families must have at least one girl and one boy, so it is permissible to have a small family, but most don't, unless the woman's health is at risk, she is very young, or nursing an infant.

The arrival of children in a Jewish home is an auspicious, and in the case of Orthodox Jews, a frequent event. There are numerous observances to mark the occasion for babies of both sexes. Historically, the arrival of a son who could assist his father in his work and wouldn't require a dowry was cause for great celebration. In recent history, though, there has been an effort to mark the arrival of a daughter with equal attention.

> *The house shall be blessed with*
> *one child of each sex.*
> BET HILLEL

The Brit Milah

Who hast hallowed us by Thy
Commandments and hast commanded us
to make our sons enter into the covenant
of Abraham our father. Even as this
child has entered into the covenant so
may he enter into the Torah, the nuptial
canopy, and into good deeds.

TRADITIONAL PRAYER

The first ceremony (or *mitzvah*) in a male child's life is the *bris* (or covenant). The event can be pretty traumatic for a mother, especially if she has not witnessed a *bris* before. It should take place eight days after the birth, assuming that the baby is in good health. Even a mention of this ritual circumcision can cause an involuntary covering of the crotch in those unfamiliar with this important tradition. The *bris* is quite a significant event, and even the most non-observant Jews will have one for a son.

The expression *brit milah* means covenant of circumcision. It is the ceremony of the removal of the foreskin from the penis. This practice comes from the biblical story of Abraham's deal with God: Abraham agreed to circumcise his son when he was born in exchange for a promise from God that

Abraham's descendants would be delivered to the Promised Land.

There is also an argument to be made for circumcision for the sake of cleanliness; a circumcised penis is less vulnerable to infection. This ceremony can be a religious event with many family members and friends in attendance, or it can be a more intimate event shared with only the closest relatives. A rabbi may participate in the service, but his presence is optional. However, a *mohel*'s presence is required. This specially-trained Jewish professional knows all the ins and outs of this ritual. A good way to find one is to check with your pediatrician, rabbi, or friends.

I tried to watch so I could remember the moment, but tears streamed down my cheeks and my milk let down when I heard him scream. I left the room and gulped down a hastily-poured beer. The second time around, I was a bit more composed and did watch. Again, tears streamed down my face but this time it was due to the poignancy of witnessing my father and father-in-law holding my son as he entered the covenant. I know of three women who became weak in the knees and one who fainted during their sons' *bris*. Though it is hard to witness, even if it isn't your flesh and blood, it is not something I would ever consider skipping.

Every male among you shall be circumcised. And ye shall be circumcised in the flesh of your foreskin, and it shall be a token of a covenant betwixt Me and you. And he that is eight days old shall be circumcised among you, every male throughout your generations.

THE BIBLE

Jewish law says that the father, if he is able, must perform the circumcision. In biblical times, perhaps that was one way to go, but now that a *mohel* may be hired to perform the *bris*, and most men are not in the least prepared to take a scalpel to their own flesh and blood, most fathers defer to him. I don't know of any men who have accepted the offer; even an urologist I know wanted nothing to do with the process, except to be in the room, when it came time for his firstborn son to be circumcised.

A godparent (or *sandek*), grandfather, or great-grandfather, is given the task of holding the child still during the procedure, with guests who can bear it, looking on. Blessings are recited by the *mohel*, the circumcision is performed, and a few drops of blood are drawn. The foreskin is traditionally buried outside, but this is not imperative. Often the baby is given a small piece of gauze soaked in kosher sacramental wine to suck on to ease the pain. The wine really just makes the baby sleepy and is a good way to quiet him for a few moments. The baby is given a Hebrew name and the following is recited:

May the parents rear this child to adulthood imbued with love of Torah and the performance of good deeds and may they escort him to the wedding canopy.
THE TALMUD

While some parents may think this is an awfully harsh way to bring the child into the Jewish faith, remember that if you choose to omit the circumcision all together, as some parents have chosen to do, and your son wishes to marry a Jew, he will need to go through a ritual circumcision before he is wed. For those who convert to Judaism and are already circumcised, a small pinprick, (no pun intended) yielding a few drops of blood, is all that's needed. A moment of pain now is well worth sparing a great deal more pain and time for recovery at a later date! Plus, it gives you a chance to get all those relatives in and out of the house for their viewing of the infant, so you can get on with raising him.

Brit ha-bah

While there has been much hullabaloo over the birth of a Jewish son for thousands of years, it is only in the recent past that the birth of a daughter has been recognized with a ceremony. Historically, a Jewish baby girl was named when her father read from the Torah for the first time after her birth, but now a baby-naming can be done in several different ways. A baby-naming is called *brit ha-bah* (covenant for a daughter) or *brit Sarah* (covenant of Sarah). This ceremony may take place in the home or at a synagogue on any day (not only eight days after the birth, like a *bris*). It may include blessings for the child, parents, and grandparents and can be presided over by a rabbi or cantor, or by family members familiar with the appropriate blessings. Many people use this as an opportunity to gather friends and family to celebrate and bless the newborn.

Our God and God of our ancestors,
sustain this child unto his parents. Let
his name be known among the Jewish
people of Israel as [recite baby's name].

TRADITIONAL PRAYER

•

Welcome little one!
Blessed may you be all your days,
all your life;
Blessed may you be
wherever you are,
In all of your comings and in
all of your goings.

TRADITIONAL PRAYER

Pidyon ha-ben

*For all the firstborn of the people
of Israel are mine, both man and beast.*

THE BIBLE

Another tradition among the more observant is the *pidyon ha-ben*. Loosely translated, *pidyon ha-ben*, means the redemption of the son. Thirty days after the birth of a firstborn son, the father buys back his son from a *kohein* (now commonly known as a Cohen, Coen, or another variation). The *koheins* were the priests of the original twelve tribes of Israel.

In the transaction to reclaim a firstborn son from the priests, a few silver dollars are symbolically used; the Bible says five silver *shekels* should be the price. Buying back the son symbolizes their release from their destiny as a servant to the priests. While many nonobservant Jews don't have any familiarity with this ritual, it is another way to mark the birth of a son as a significant event.

These selected *Mitzvot* pertain to the very important role the *kohein* played in Judaism's earliest days. Several of the *Mitzvot* address how arduous a life the priests had to live.

* To give the first of the fleece to the *kohein*

* To set apart *t'rumah g'dolah* (the great leave-offering, that is, a small portion of the grain, wine, and oil) for the *kohein*

* That the *kohanim* shall put on priestly vestments for the service

* Not to tear the High *Kohein's* robe

* That the *kohanim* defile themselves for their deceased relatives (by attending their burial), and mourn for them like other Israelites, who are commanded to mourn for their relatives

* That a *kohein* shall not marry a divorced woman

* That a *kohein* shall not marry a harlot

* That a *kohein* shall not marry a profaned woman

* To show honor to a *kohein*, and to give him precedence in all things that are holy

* That the High *Kohein* shall marry a virgin

* That the High *Kohein* shall not marry a widow

* That the High *Kohein* shall not cohabit with a widow, even without marriage, because he profanes her

* That a *kohein* who is unclean shall not serve (in the Sanctuary)

* That the *kohanim* shall bless Israel

* To set apart a portion of the dough for the *kohein*

* That a person who is not a *kohein* or the wife or unmarried daughter of a *kohein* shall not eat of the *t'rumah*

* That the High *Kohein* shall offer a meal offering daily

* To decide in regard to dedicated property as to which is sacred to the Lord and which belongs to the *kohein*

* That the *kohanim* shall not eat the flesh of the sin-offering or guilt-offering outside the Courtyard (of the Sanctuary)

The Bar or Bat Mitzvah

On the occasion of a *Bar* or *Bat Mitzvah*:

*One should endeavor to make a feast for
dear ones and friends and invite Torah
scholars and have much feasting and joy
according to the hand of God upon him
for this meal will be a great defense
upon Israel*

RABBI YOSEF CHAIM

This ceremony is arguably the most significant
event in a Jewish child's life. Literally translated,
Bar (or *Bat*) means "a son (or daughter) of the
Commandments," meaning that at the age of thirteen,
a young man or woman must now abide by the
Commandments. Prior to that time, a child is learning
the Commandments and should begin to understand
what will be expected of him or her as a Jewish adult.
There is no explicit directive in the Torah or the
Talmud regarding this event except that he or she must
now obey the Commandments. The age of thirteen
may have been designated as the age at which young
Jewish men must observe the *Mitzvot* because it was the
time at which Jacob and Esau separated, and when
Abraham rejected idol worship. It is also a time when
the father is no longer expected to oversee his child's

Torah study. At the age of thirteen, the young person assumes responsibility for his or her own study.

If he or she neglects Torah studies, the father will bear no spiritual punishment. The following prayer formally exempts the father and is often recited at the celebration:

Blessed is he that has acquitted me from this person's punishment.

BERESHIT RABAH

•

Correct your child and he will give you rest; yea, he will give delight unto your soul.

THE TALMUD

The *Bar* or *Bat Mitzvah* marks a child's entrance into adulthood. At one time, it was only celebrated by boys; now Jewish girls can choose to have a *Bat Mitzvah* as well. At the age of twelve for girls and a year later for boys, *B'nai Mitzvah* are to become more active participants in the Jewish community. Boys may be counted toward a *minyan* (a prayer quorum of ten), and they may begin to lay *tefillin* (prayer aids) and fully participate in religious services. For girls, it is the age when they start to learn how to keep a home and refine their knowledge of domestic tasks, although this seems somewhat dated now. Perhaps it is best thought of as a time when a Jewish girl may consider herself responsible for following the same *Mitzvot* that boys are required to observe. The *Bat Mitzvah* is a recent addition to the Jewish life cycle; the first Jewish woman to be a *Bat Mitzvah* was Judith Kaplan, the daughter of the founder of the Jewish Reconstructionist movement who celebrated hers on March 18, 1922.

It is assumed that a child who wishes to become a *Bar* or *Bat Mitzvah* will attend religious school and learn to read and understand Hebrew. There is less emphasis on the conversational elements of the language, though often children with an interest in speaking it can attend additional classes. It is expected that the child will be called for his or her first *aliyah* (honor) and will read from the Torah and *Haftorah*, as well as conduct part of the service. Obviously, the more observant the family, the more significant a role the child will play in the service and the more Hebrew he or she will be expected to read. Most American synagogues require attendance at religious school in order to have a service in the sanctuary, but there are many rabbis who will perform the service at another venue, such as your country club, favorite restaurant, or mother-in-law's mah-jongg club.

The Divine word spoke to each and every person according to his or her capacity: the young according to their capacity and the old in keeping with their capacity.

THE MIDRASH

•

Blessed is the one who has freed me from responsibility from this one.

TRADITIONAL PRAYER

When I was a *Bat Mitzvah*, I was not what you would call a diligent student and struggled to learn and commit to memory my Torah portion. In desperation, I resorted to writing the transliteration of the one prayer I could not seem to get right on a tiny piece of paper in tiny letters. I folded the piece of paper into an even smaller square and tucked the crib sheet into the pocket of my dress. Upon reaching the *bimah* (the stage from which the service is led), I surreptitiously pulled it from my pocket and read it flawlessly, to the amazement of my parents. The ensuing festivities notwithstanding, I do regret to this day that I wasn't more focused on the purpose of the service. Had I been a bit more mature, I would have spent a lot more time learning my prayers and a lot less time concerned about whether I would receive the hot bracelet at the time with my name on it as a gift or whether the cute boy I liked would pay

attention to me at my pool party the next day. Though many *B'nai Mitzvah* are unable to grasp the true meaning and importance of the day, a little more prodding about adequate preparation and the big picture and a little less attention to the DJ's playlist and the color of the party favors, would help everyone keep the entire event in proper perspective. *Bar* and *Bat Mitzvahs* are a religious ceremony, first and foremost, and a little restraint is a good thing.

A *Bar* or *Bat Mitzvah* is expected to observe each of the 613 *Mitzvot* once he or she becomes a "son (or daughter) of the Commandments." These pertain to how a Jew should treat his fellow man and act charitably. Many Talmudic scholars suggest that these laws provide a moral compass in an increasingly complicated world. While we may not need guidance on the bartering of a heifer, or whether seeds of different crops may be sown in the same field, many of these *Mitzvot* provide a valuable set of guidelines for anyone; Jewish, Christian, Muslim, young or old.

* Not to refrain from maintaining a poor man and giving him what he needs
* To give charity according to one's means
* To love the stranger
* Not to wrong the stranger in speech
* Not to wrong the stranger in buying or selling
* Not to intermarry with gentiles
* To lend to an alien at interest
* To exact the debt of an alien
* Not to do wrong in buying or selling
* Not to make a loan to an Israelite on interest
* Not to borrow on interest
* Not to take part in any usurious transaction between borrower and lender, neither as a surety, nor as a witness, nor as a writer of the bond for them
* That a hired laborer shall not eat produce that is not being harvested
* To pay wages to the hired man at the due time
* To deal judicially with the Hebrew bondman in accordance with the laws appertaining to him
* Not to muzzle a beast, while it is working in produce which it can eat and enjoy
* That a man should fulfill whatever he has uttered

* Not to swear needlessly
* Not to violate an oath or swear falsely
* To decide in cases of annulment of vows, according to the rules set forth in the Torah
* Not to break a vow
* To swear by His name truly
* Not to delay in fulfilling vows or bringing vowed or free-will offerings
* To appoint judges and officers in every community of Israel
* Not to appoint as a judge a person who is not well versed in the laws of the Torah, even if he is expert in other branches of knowledge
* To adjudicate cases of purchase and sale
* To lend to a poor person
* Not to demand from a poor man repayment of his debt, when the creditor knows that he cannot pay, nor press him
* Not to take in pledge utensils used in preparing food
* Not to exact a pledge from a debtor by force
* Not to keep the pledge from its owner at the time when he needs it
* To return a pledge to its owner

* Not to take a pledge from a widow
* Not to commit fraud in measuring
* To ensure that scales and weights are correct
* Not to possess inaccurate measures and weights
* Not to delay payment of a hired man's wages
* That the hired laborer shall be permitted to eat of the produce he is reaping
* That the hired laborer shall not take more than he can eat

Death

*And he made a mourning for his father
seven days.*

Judaism has always maintained that death is part of life, not a separate event. Death must be recognized according to tradition, and even honored. Euphemisms like "passing away" or "the loss" of someone are discouraged since they lessen the impact of a death and might even ease the pain of grieving. The individual has died, not left, and hasn't gone off to a better place—acknowledging that is a requirement of Jewish mourning.

Jews regardless of their affiliation with a synagogue will often call a rabbi when a loved one has died. The Jewish community's response is an integral part of the mourning process: Support, a *minyan* when sitting *shiva*, counseling, guidance, and providing assistance with the funeral are all part of the process of burying the dead.

*Jacob rent his garments and placed
sackcloth on his loins; he mourned for his
son many days.*

80   THE GOOD JEWISH HOME

Jews believe that the burial should take place as soon as possible after death. Funerals are not held on *Shabbat* or holidays and are often put off for at most a day to allow family to gather. The body should not be left alone before the funeral, and family and friends and often funeral home employees remain with the deceased until burial. There are no open caskets or wakes. The casket, after it has been lowered into the ground, is often covered with handfuls of dirt thrown in by mourners; this assures that the family understands that death has occurred.

The basis of Jewish mourning is related to the belief that the body should be returned to the earth quickly and naturally. Embalming, which slows the process of decomposition is not done; the body should be allowed to break down organically. The body is carefully washed, dressed in a plain white shroud, and placed in a simple pine box with handles. Despite the popularity of elaborate caskets, Jewish law states that a plain box be used. Outside the United States, Jews are often laid to rest without a casket. Burial underground is required, cremation is prohibited in observant families, and a consecrated Jewish cemetery is the only appropriate place. A tombstone is placed at the head of the gravesite; this is meant to be a reminder of the dead so he or she will not be forgotten. When people visit the grave, they often leave a small stone on the tombstone as a sign that they have been there. Just as the stone lasts forever, so too does the soul live forever. It is traditional to erect a tombstone on the first anniversary of death; during the first year the dead are mourned each day so no reminder is required. The unveiling of the tombstone is attended by family and close friends, and is a relatively new custom.

Jews are usually buried with family within the community, or as close as feasible. The intention is that they remain near their surviving loved ones and still be a part of the community after death.

I acknowledge before You that my life and death are in Your hands. May it be Your will to heal me. But if death is my lot, then I accept it from Your hand with love. May my death be atonement for whatever sins and errors and wrong doings I have committed before You.

TRADITIONAL PRAYER

Sitting Shiva

The process of sitting *shiva* (seven) and how closely the laws of mourning are followed depends on the family's level of observance. Often, those who are not particularly religious will adhere closely to the laws of mourning because it can be a tremendous comfort during a difficult time. For seven days after death, the family will mourn at home.

They can do some or all of the following:

* Mourners sit on boxes or footstools. Any item may do as long as it is lower than the usual resting place. Sephardic Jews follow the tradition of sitting on the floor. This is a literal translation of feeling low or sad.

* Leather shoes are not worn.

* Male mourners do not shave.

* Mourners may not go to work for the week of *shiva*.

* There may be no pleasure during these seven days: no sex, listening to music, playing an instrument, or even doing laundry.

* Garments are rent; in contemporary society, a small black pin with a bit of torn ribbon is worn over the heart.

* Mirrors in the place of mourning are covered; this serves as a reminder that vanity is unimportant at this time.

* A *minyan* must be present to say a *Kaddish* (traditional Jewish prayer of mourning); ten men who are familiar with the prayers can plan to be at the home of the deceased in advance.

* Freely weeping and expressing grief is not only acceptable but required.

Friends and family play an important role in helping someone grieve. The condolence call simply means that the survivors receive guests at home during *shiva* and traditionally are brought food so that they do not need to prepare any meals. The visit is meant to be a solemn one; sharing memories of the deceased is appropriate, gossiping and socializing is not. All these guidelines are meant to allow the survivors the opportunity to focus on their mourning and grief. A week of immersion into the mourning process allows it to truly sink in. After the week is over, returning to a normal schedule should be easier.

I acknowledge before You, O Lord my God and God of my fathers, that my life and death are in Your hands. May it be Your will to heal me. But if death is my lot, then I accept it and wrong doings I have committed before You. In Your mercy grant me the goodness that is waiting for the righteous and bring me to eternal life. Father of orphans, Protector of widows, protect my loved ones with whom my soul is bound. Into Your hands I return my spirit. You will redeem me, O ever faithful God. Hear O Israel, the Lord is God, the Lord is One.

PRAYER BOOK

Yahrzeit

Yahrzeit, or the first year anniversary of a death, is observed when a parent or child has died, with the lighting of a twenty-four hour candle. This light is meant to memorialize the dead and one is also lit on Yom Kippur (the Day of Atonement). The *yahrzeit* candle should be illuminated after dark on the evening before the anniversary of the death. Many people visit the graves of the deceased on the *yahrzeit*. The person observing the anniversary of a loved one's death is also called the *yahrzeit*. The candle's purpose is interpreted in the following text:

> *The soul of man is the lamp of God.*
> THE BIBLE

While Jews have observed *yahrzeit* (a Yiddish word) since Talmudic times, the ceremony wasn't called *yahrzeit* until the 16th century. The word comes from the German word *Jahrzeit*, a word used by the Christian Church for the occasion of honoring the dead. It is a tradition, not a law, but provides a chance to remember a loved one with a simple act.

Let the Glory of God be exalted, let God's
great name be hallowed in the world
whose creation God willed. May God's
rule soon prevail, in our own day, our
own lives, and the life of all Israel, and
let us say: Amen

Let God's great name be blessed forever
and ever.

Let the name of the Holy One, blessed is
God, be glorified, exalted, and honored,
though God is beyond all the praises,
songs, and adorations that are uttered in
this world, and let us say: Amen.

May there be abundant peace from
heaven, and life for us and all Israel, and
let us say: Amen.

May the one who makes peace in the
high heavens make peace descend on us
and upon all Israel, and let us say:
Amen.

MOURNER'S KADDISH

Chapter Three

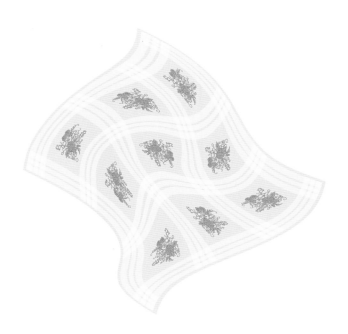

THE JEWISH YEAR

The Jewish calendar, often a source of confusion for non-Jews, follows the lunar calendar, not the Gregorian (or solar) calendar used by most of the Western world. The lunar year is not the same length as the solar year, which means that holidays will rarely fall on the same day they did the year prior. A line often heard before the High Holy Days of Rosh Hashanah and Yom Kippur is "this year the holidays are early" or "this year the holidays are late." Our family likes to joke that the holidays fall on time; only early or late!

On the Jewish calendar, each new month begins on *Rosh Chodesh* (the new moon) when the first sliver of moon becomes visible after dark. In biblical times, the new months were determined by when the moon was seen with the naked eye. When people observed the new moon, they would notify the *Sanhedrin* (seventy-one Torah scholars, sort of like a Jewish Supreme Court). When the *Sanhedrin* heard testimony from two independent, reliable eyewitnesses that the new moon was observed, they would announce the arrival of the *Rosh Chodesh* and send out messengers to tell people when the month began. This explains the seemingly erratic arrival of the variety of Jewish holidays.

From one new moon to another, and from one Sabbath to another, shall all flesh come to worship before Me saith the Lord.

THE BIBLE

•

Also in the day of your gladness, and in your appointed seasons, and in your new moons, ye shall blow with the trumpets over your burnt offerings

THE BIBLE

Jewish holidays are serious stuff. Some require fasting and a lot of time at synagogue; others demand great merrymaking, and still others warrant charitable acts. While some Commandments dictate exactly how to observe certain holidays, practicality and modern living have made it harder to follow the rules exactly. For example, it might be a challenge to find an acceptable spot to sacrifice a Paschal lamb on Passover (not to mention the inconvenience of locating a lamb, should you live in a city), so the placement of a lamb shank on the Seder plate may serve as an adequate substitute. Judaism requires that you make your best efforts to observe and celebrate the Sabbath and holidays; beyond that is a personal decision. A young man far away from home and with no wife or children may find it harder to celebrate

Rosh Hashanah, but when he has settled down he may find great pleasure in celebrating the holidays with his family.

The guidelines for how Jews should conduct themselves on holy days are written in the 613 *Mitzvot*:

* That the new month shall be solemnly proclaimed as holy, and the months and years shall be calculated by the Supreme Court only

* Not to travel on *Shabbat* outside the limits of one's place of residence

* To sanctify *Shabbat*

* Not to do work on *Shabbat*

* To rest on *Shabbat*

* To celebrate the festivals (Passover, *Shavuot*, and *Sukkot*)

* To rejoice on the festivals

* To appear in the Sanctuary on the festivals

* To remove *chametz* on the Eve of Passover

* To rest on the first day of Passover

* Not to do work on the first day of Passover

* To rest on the seventh day of Passover

* Not to do work on the seventh day of Passover

* To eat matzoh on the first night of Passover

* That no *chametz* be in the Israelite's possession during Passover

* Not to eat any food containing *chametz* on Passover

* Not to eat *chametz* on Passover

* That *chametz* shall not be seen in an Israelite's home during Passover

* To discuss the departure from Egypt on the first night of Passover

* Not to eat *chametz* after mid-day on the fourteenth of *Nisan*

* To count forty-nine days from the time of the cutting of the *Omer* (first sheaves of the barley harvest)

* To rest on *Shavuot*

* Not to do work on the *Shavuot*

* To rest on Rosh Hashanah

* Not to do work on Rosh Hashanah

* To hear the sound of the *shofar* on Rosh Hashanah

* To fast on Yom Kippur

* Not to eat or drink on Yom Kippur

* Not to do work on Yom Kippur

* To rest on Yom Kippur

* To rest on the first day of *Sukkot*

* Not to do work on the first day of *Sukkot*

* To rest on the eighth day of *Sukkot* (*Shemini Atzeret*)

* Not to do work on the eighth day of *Sukkot* (*Shemini Atzeret*)

Shabbat

Come, my dear friend, to meet the bride,
the Sabbath Presence let us welcome.

RABBI SHLOMO ALKABETZ

The *Shabbat* starts on Friday evening at sunset and ends at sunset on Saturday, when at least three stars are visible. It is observed by Jews worldwide in many ways. Jews are meant to set aside this day to rest, share time with family, recognize the miracle of life and the world around us, and step off the treadmill that society has us racing upon. One of the Ten Commandments states that we should honor the Sabbath. There are no specific directives as to how the day should be spent, but there are many that tell us how not to spend the day. The Talmud tells us there are thirty-nine categories of *melachah* (work) that are forbidden on the Sabbath. These include any tasks that would have been associated with the construction of the portable Temple which was moved when the Jews were wandering the desert. Cooking, grinding, laundry, knitting, sewing, construction repairs, writing, building a fire, hunting, fishing, and planting are all examples of prohibited work. Observant Jews will not turn on lights, operate any machinery from a pencil sharpener to a car, cook, clean, use money, transact business, or conduct themselves as they would on other day. *Shabbos goys* (non-Jewish helpers) are often retained to assist with the tasks that must be done. Elevator buttons in buildings where observant Jews reside will often have settings to use on the Sabbath so residents will not have to press anything. Even my oven has a Sabbath setting to turn itself off and on for preparing food after the sun has set on Friday. While many people may find these guidelines restrictive, an observant Jew welcomes this opportunity to rest and recharge.

For six days labor may be done and the seventh day is a day of complete rest, a holy convocation, you shall not do any work. It is a Sabbath for Hashem (God) in all your dwelling places.

THE BIBLE

•

He who delights in the Sabbath is granted his heart's desire.

THE TALMUD

Israel is to keep the Sabbath so that its animals and workers might rest, even during the harvest, and because God, who liberated it from Egyptian bondage, so commanded it.

THE BIBLE

•

Whoever keeps the Sabbath testifies of Him at whose word the world came into being; that He created the world in six days and rested on the seventh.

SIMEON BAR YOHAI

•

Many of those unfamiliar with Jewish law question under what circumstances may one make an exception to the observance of Shabbat. When a human life is in danger, the laws may be temporarily disregarded. This means if someone is deathly ill and it is after sunset on Friday, they may be driven to the hospital. A sick child may see a doctor and a phone may be used to call the police or fire department if there is imminent danger.
Desecrate one Shabbat so that one may live to celebrate many.

THE TALMUD

Despite the many restrictions placed on Jews when observing of the Sabbath, families should celebrate the day in a way that brings them together joyfully. Many families gather for a festive dinner that includes traditional dishes, songs, and prayers and then return to their busy lives the following morning. Many choose to attend *Shabbat* services at their synagogue or light candles and say the prayers over the wine and *challah*. Tradition calls for the presence of two *challahs*; they represent the double portion of manna that rained from Heaven before *Shabbat* arrived so the Jews would not have to prepare or gather food once *Shabbat* had arrived.

Call the Sabbath a delight and thou shalt honor it.

ISAIAH

•

A precious jewel I have in my possession which I wish to give to Israel, and Sabbath is its name.

THE MIDRASH

•

If Israel keeps one Sabbath as it should be kept, the Messiah will come. The Sabbath is equal to all the other precepts of the Torah.

THE BIBLE

A word about Jews and food: Jewish food is an integral part of the celebration and observance of every Jewish holiday. Even Yom Kippur, the day on which we fast and deprive ourselves of the pleasure of eating, is ended with a breaking of the fast. The food we eat to break our fast has traditionally been the same for generations. The memories we have of certain foods are forever linked with family, holidays, and celebrations. When family is gathered, the Bible tells us, the food will always be delicious.

A traditional *Shabbat* meal is usually a substantial one. The menu often includes matzoh ball soup or other *mandlen* (dumplings), a roasted chicken or brisket, a vegetable, and a potato dish. Historically, Jews prepared a stewlike dish of meat, barley, spices, and potatoes called *cholent* that was prepared and placed in the oven before sunset and could simmer for as long as necessary. It could be eaten at any point during the twenty-four hour period and was often cooked in a communal oven in a *cholent* pot, which is set aside specifically for that purpose.

*Better is a dinner of herbs where love is,
than a fatted ox and hatred with it.*
THE BIBLE

GEFILTE FISH

Gefilte fish is a traditional *Shabbat* dish. Fish was expensive in Eastern Europe so it was ground and mixed with less costly ingredients like bread, eggs, onions, and sugar. Preparing gefilte fish from scratch is a fairly complex undertaking. Luckily, preprepared gefilte fish may be bought from a kosher butcher shop, so making this dish yourself is not essential for a traditional observance of *Shabbat*. Should you prefer to prepare it yourself, here is a family recipe.

1½ pounds whitefish

1½ pounds pike

3 medium onions, peeled and sliced thin

3 medium carrots, peeled and sliced thin

2 parsnips, peeled and sliced thin

2 stalks celery, trimmed and sliced thin

1 egg

1 teaspoon granulated sugar

1 tablespoon breadcrumbs or unseasoned matzoh meal

1 teaspoon salt

¼ teaspoon freshly ground pepper

Clean, fillet, and lightly salt fish the night before, and chill. Set aside the bones and skin. Fill a large pot with a quart of water and add two of the onions, the carrots, parsnips, and celery. Add fish bones and skin and boil for about 10 minutes.

Chop the fish and the remaining onion on a large cutting board until it has a consistency of a thick paste. Place in a large bowl and add egg, sugar, breadcrumbs, salt, and pepper. Fish should be sticky to the touch.

Form mixture into patties, adding a few more breadcrumbs as needed to help them adhere. Drop the patties carefully into the boiling water. Salt the water lightly. Boil, covered, over low heat for 2 hours, then uncover and boil another ½ hour. Remove from heat, set aside, and allow to cool.

Refrigerate after cooling and serve with freshly grated horseradish root and sliced beets.

Serves 12

CHICKEN SOUP WITH MATZOH BALLS

1 four-pound whole stewing hen, or other chicken

4 quarts cold water

2 medium carrots, peeled and trimmed

1 large onion, peeled

2 medium parsnips, peeled and trimmed

2 ribs celery with leaves, trimmed

1 tablespoon chopped fresh dill (optional)

Salt and white pepper to taste

Rinse the chicken inside and out, setting aside the giblets for another use or discard. If you wish, add the neck to the soup and save the liver for chopped liver. Place in a large stock pot. Fill with the cold water and bring to a boil over high heat. After it has rapidly boiled for a few minutes, skim foam off the top as well as any other bits that have floated to the surface.

Reduce to medium heat and add carrot, onion, and parsnip and cover. Boil for about 30 minutes. Reduce heat and simmer for about 2 hours, then turn off heat. Remove chicken carefully, draining soup from cavity over pot and place in bowl. When cool enough to handle, remove skin, bones, and cartilage and discard. Remove vegetables, thinly slice, and return to pot. Season with salt and white pepper to taste. Add some chicken pieces back and dill, if desired.

Allow pot to cool completely, cover, and place in refrigerator. The next day, use a large spoon to remove accumulated fat on the top and discard. Reheat thoroughly and serve.

Serves 8 to 10 (depending on bowl size)

MATZOH BALLS

3 large eggs, well beaten

4 tablespoon melted schmaltz (chicken fat)

¾ cup unseasoned matzoh meal

1 teaspoon salt, plus pinch more to taste

Pour beaten eggs into medium bowl and add chicken fat. Mix well, and then add matzoh meal and salt. Mix well again with a fork, breaking up any lumps. Place in refrigerator for ½ hour, covered loosely.

Bring a large pot of salted water to a rolling boil and take out bowl of moistened matzoh meal. Form small balls (a little smaller than a golf ball) with your hands; the mixture will be very sticky. Drop into the boiling water. When all the mixture has been used, cover pot with a tightly fitting lid, reduce heat, and simmer for ½ hour.

Using a slotted spoon, remove matzoh balls carefully from pot and place in nonreactive casserole dish lined with a paper towel, if serving later.

If serving immediately, drop matzoh balls into soup. Salt again, if desired, to taste.

Makes about 12 small or 10 medium matzoh balls

LECHA DODI

Lecha Dodi,
Likrat Kala, Likrat Kala,
Penei Shabbat n'kab'la, n'kab'la.

Shabbat Shalom (repeat)
Shabbat shalom umevorach.

Translation:
Come My Beloved

Come my beloved
to meet the bride,
Let us welcome the Sabbath.

A Sabbath of peace,
Blessed Sabbath.

BEEF BRISKET
FOR SHABBAT

2 tablespoons vegetable oil

4 large onions, sliced thin

One 4-pound beef brisket

2 cloves garlic, crushed

2 tablespoons all-purpose flour

Salt and freshly ground pepper to taste

1 teaspoon paprika

1 small can tomato paste, preferably imported

4 carrots, peeled

Preheat oven to 325°F. Place Dutch oven over a low flame and add oil. When oil is hot but not smoking, add onions and sauté until soft and fragrant. While onions are cooking, rinse brisket with water and pat dry with a paper towel. Rub the meat on all sides with crushed garlic and flour, and sprinkle with salt, pepper, and paprika. Remove onions from Dutch oven and set aside.

Put meat in Dutch oven and brown on all sides. Remove from heat, and spread tomato paste over meat as if frosting a cake. Add carrots, cover, and place in oven. After 1½ hours, remove from oven and place meat on a heavy carving board. Carve thinly on the diagonal against the grain, then reassemble and return to pot.

Cook again for another 1½ hours, adding a ½ cup of water if needed. Slice carrots and serve with meat. Gravy may be made with the juices at the bottom of the pan. Pour liquid into a small pan, scraping up any accumulated bits from the bottom. Heat and season liquid to taste, straining off excess fat.

Serves 6 to 8

SEPHARDIC ROAST CHICKEN

One 6- to 6 ½-pound roasting chicken,
preferably kosher

2 tablespoons olive oil

1½ teaspoons ground cumin

1 teaspoon garlic powder

1 teaspoon onion powder

1 teaspoon paprika

½ teaspoon salt

½ teaspoon freshly ground black pepper

1 large lemon, halved

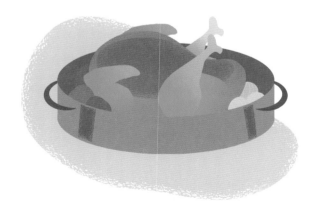

Preheat oven to 375°F. Rinse the chicken inside and out and pat dry. Place chicken on rack in large roasting pan.

Stir oil, cumin, garlic and onion powders, paprika, salt, and pepper in small bowl to form paste. Rub spice paste all over chicken.

Roast chicken for 1 hour. Remove chicken from oven and squeeze juice from lemon halves over chicken; place lemon halves inside main cavity. Place back in oven and continue to roast until chicken is cooked through and thermometer inserted into thickest part of thigh registers 175°F, about 1 hour longer. Transfer to platter; let stand 15 minutes.

Meanwhile, pour roasting pan drippings into a small saucepan. Scrape in any remaining bits from the roasting pan. Heat over low flame, stirring occasionally. Season with salt and pepper to taste. When serving, spoon off top layer of oil from gravy.

Serves 4 to 6

TRADITIONAL APPLE CAKE

Apples are a favorite Jewish dessert ingredient. They figure prominently in Rosh Hashanah recipes and are symbolic of the harvest and the season. With good baking apples readily available year round and in every grocer, cooks are not limited to preparing this dish only in the fall.

3 cups unbleached all-purpose flour

Pinch salt

1 tablespoon baking powder

4 large Granny Smith apples, peeled, cored, and cut into thick slices

Juice of ½ lemon

4 large eggs

1 cup vegetable oil

2 cups sugar

1 tablespoon pure vanilla extract

½ cup orange juice

1 teaspoon ground cinnamon

Preheat the oven to 350°F. Lightly grease with oil a 9-inch springform pan. Mix the flour, salt, and baking powder in a bowl and set aside. Place apple slices in a bowl and sprinkle with lemon juice to keep from browning. In another bowl, beat the eggs well and add the vegetable oil, 1¾ cups of the sugar and vanilla, and mix well.

Add the dry ingredients and the orange juice to the beaten egg mixture. Pour half the batter into the prepared pan. Cover with half the sliced apples.

In a small bowl, mix the remaining ¼ cup sugar with the cinnamon and sprinkle over the apples. Cover with the rest of the batter. Place the remaining apple slices in a circle on top of the batter.

Bake for 1¼ hours, or until a toothpick inserted in the cake comes out clean. Cool on a rack before removing from the pan.

Serves 12

FRUITY SWEET POTATO TZIMMES

4 large sweet potatoes or yams, peeled, and cut into 1-inch cubes

1 pound assorted dried fruit, preferably prunes, apricots, and peaches

¾ cup orange juice

¼ cup honey

¼ cup packed brown sugar

1 teaspoon ground cinnamon

½ teaspoon ginger

Preheat oven to 375°F. Combine all ingredients and place in greased 2-quart baking dish or 9- by 13-inch pan.

Cover tightly and bake for 1½ hours, until vegetables are tender and fruit is soft. Stir before serving.

Serves 8

VARIATION: Substitute in place of dried fruit 4 large carrots, peeled, trimmed, and sliced.

The Holidays

ROSH HASHANAH

It is the custom of men who appear before a court of justice to wear black clothes, to let their beards grow long because the outcome is uncertain. But Israel does not do so. On the 'Day of Judgment ('Rosh Ha-Shanah), they wear white garments and have their beards shaven and they eat, drink, and rejoice in the conviction that God will perform miracles for them.

TALMUD YERUSHALMI

The Jewish New Year, Rosh Hashanah, is celebrated in the fall shortly before the observance of Yom Kippur. These two holidays are called the High Holy Days or the Days of Awe and are the most significant observances on the Jewish calendar. Rosh Hashanah marks the day the year number changes, not the first day of the calendar year.

This holiday is marked by the blowing of the *shofar*, the horn of any animal but a cow. This is a particularly difficult task to accomplish; those who can blow it well are accorded great respect. The sounding of the *shofar* in the synagogue is an occasion of great solemnity during which God is asked to show mercy to His creatures. But there is nothing wrong with children greeting the sounds of the *shofar* with gleeful shouts.

This holiday gives us a chance to start anew. We can free ourselves from feelings of failure and disappointment, anger toward someone else, or hostility toward something or someone who has let us down. An inscription in the "book of life" is not literal; Jews don't die because they have failed somehow, they die because they are old, sick, or injured. A Jew can be written into the "book of death" by carrying negative feelings and behaviors into the next year. There are no actual books, just a chance to start again with a clear conscience.

Rosh Hashanah begins after sunset the night before (*erev*) as all Jewish holidays do and lasts for two days. Most Jews attend synagogue the evening the holiday begins and the following morning.

A ritual called *tashlich* (thou shalt cast) is a symbolic opportunity to cast out one's sins and begin the New Year with a fresh outlook. Jews travel to a body of running water, or to a well if no running water is nearby, and repeat a set of prayers specific to *tashlich*. Participants empty their pockets of crumbs and bits of lint and cast them into the water as a symbol of their failures. If your pockets are already empty, breadcrumbs are a fine substitute.

Traditionally, sweet foods are eaten to symbolize the desire for a sweet year; apples and honey are placed on the table and each person is invited to eat a piece. A round *challah*, customarily eaten on this and other holidays and celebrations, may even be studded with raisins. Other traditional foods for Rosh Hashanah are like those eaten on the Sabbath. Food prepared with honey has become a tradition as well, especially honey cake and cookies. Apples are a favorite Jewish dessert ingredient. They figure prominently in Rosh Hashanah recipes and are symbolic of the harvest and the season.

HONEY CAKE

4 eggs

1 cup granulated sugar & 1 cup brown sugar

6 tablespoons vegetable oil

1 pound honey (softened)

1 cup warm coffee

2 tablespoons orange juice

1 tablespoon grated orange zest

5½ cups all-purpose flour

2 teaspoons each baking powder &
   baking soda

2 teaspoons ground cinnamon

2 teaspoons allspice

1 cup coarsely chopped almonds or walnuts

Preheat oven to 325°F. Place honey bottle in bowl of warm water, about ½ hour before using to soften.

Beat eggs well in a large bowl. Add sugars, oil, honey, coffee, orange juice, and rind. Stir flour, baking powder, baking soda, cinnamon, and allspice together in a medium bowl.

Gradually add flour mixture to wet ingredients. Mix well, then add chopped nuts and mix again.

Pour batter into two greased loaf pans and bake for 1 hour.

Makes 2 loaves (This recipe may be halved for 1 loaf.)

DATE AND APPLE TART

3 tablespoons butter (or margarine)

8 small Granny Smith apples (about 3 pounds), peeled, cored, and cut into 12 slices

⅓ cup plus 2 tablespoons honey

Prepared pie crust, defrosted

⅔ cup chopped assorted nuts (preferably walnuts and almonds)

5 large pitted dates, slivered

Preheat oven to 400°F. Melt butter in heavy large skillet over medium-high heat. Add apples and sauté until brown and soft, about 15 minutes. Reduce heat to medium and pour ⅓ cup honey over apples. Gently mix in honey and remove from heat. Set aside.

Fit crust onto a rimless baking sheet lined with a round of parchment paper and sprinkle with nuts. Press down with a flat spatula to embed nuts in crust. Spoon three-quarters of the apple mixture over crust but leave a 2-inch space between crust edge and filling. Sprinkle dates over apples and then add rest of apple mixture. Fold edges of crust over apples to seal in sides.

Bake tart until crust begins to brown, about 15 minutes. Reduce heat to 375°F and bake until crust is golden brown, about 10 minutes longer. Loosen tart from parchment paper with spatula. Cool on baking sheet until warm, about 45 minutes.

Serves 8

Although it is a divine decree that we blow the shofar on Rosh Ha-Shanah, a hint of the following idea is contained in the command. It is as if to say: 'Awake from your slumbers, ye who have fallen asleep in life, and reflect on your deeds.' Look well to your souls and improve your character. Forsake each of you his evil ways and thoughts.

MAIMONIDES

•

Recite before Me on Rosh Ha-Shanah malkhuyyot, zikhronot, and shofarot: Malkhuyyot so that you may proclaim Me King over you; zikhronot so that your remembrance may rise favorably before Me; and through what? Through the shofar.

TALMUDIC TRACTATE ROSH HA-SHANAH

•

May you be inscribed (in the "book of life") for a good year.

TRADITIONAL SAYING

Swinging the chicken?

While most Jewish traditions are solemn, especially those associated with the Days of Awe, there is one that will inevitably generate a giggle from even the most serious. As a child hearing about the *kapparot* ritual, I was sure I was being teased.

This ritual is performed on the last day before Yom Kippur; it involves the swinging of a live chicken over one's head three times—roosters for men and hens for women. The animal is then slaughtered and given to the poor who might not have a chicken with which to feed their family. The chicken is meant to serve as a substitute and assume the misfortune that might meet the swinger. Clearly the basis for this somewhat bizarre custom is charity. Many Jews who want to participate but may not be able to get their hands around a live chicken choose to swing a small bag of coins instead and give that to the needy. There is no biblical precedent for this ritual; it is first mentioned in an ancient scholarly text.

> *This is my substitute, my vicarious offering, my atonement; this fowl shall meet death, but I shall find a long and pleasant life of peace.*
>
> TRADITIONAL PRAYER

Yom Kippur

For on this day shall atonement be made for you, to cleanse you; from all your sins shall ye be clean before the Lord.

THE TORAH

The Day of Atonement, as this holiday is called, is the most solemn day on the Jewish calendar. It comes at the end of the ten-day period known as the Days of Awe. It is a day set aside for introspection, prayer, self-deprivation, forgiveness, setting aside grudges, letting go of vengeful feelings, and a chance for spiritual renewal. Fasting is traditional; children under thirteen years old, pregnant women, the elderly, and sick are exempt. It is customary to wish fellow congregants an easy fast on this holiday instead of using a more festive greeting.

The day is meant to be spent at synagogue, praying, thinking, reflecting, but not socializing or doing anything that yields pleasure, including having sex, luxurious bathing, or recreation. Much like mourning, the intent is to deprive yourself of the usual comforts so that you can better focus on the important things for this solemn day.

The holiday begins the evening before (*erev*). This evening is called *Kol Nidre* (all vows), and is named for the hauntingly beautiful prayer sung at the evening service. The worshipers proclaim that all personal vows, oaths, promises, and obligations they made unwittingly, rashly, or unknowingly during the year should be considered null and void.

This shall be to you a law for all time; to make atonement for all the Israelites for all their sins once a year.

THE TORAH

•

To observe, on Yom Kippur, the service appointed for that day, regarding the sacrifice, confessions, sending away of the scapegoat, etc.

A MITZVAH

The twenty-five hour period that is Yom Kippur is broken into sections determined by parts of the day. The *Kol Nidre* service, held the night before, is but the beginning; the following morning, perhaps with smelling salts in hand to ward off dizziness and an empty stomach, Jews gather at the synagogue again.

This service or the *Sachri,* extends through the morning and is sometimes followed by the *Musaf* service (added on *Shabbat*), then by the *Minchah* service, and finally by the closing or concluding service called the *Neilah.* Usually before the concluding service there is a memorial service (or *Yizkor*) for those who have lost members of their immediate families. Some Jews are superstitious and will send children out of the synagogue before the service begins and generally those who have not lost parents or children do not attend. This is a very moving and spiritual service so for those who want to stay there is no prohibition on remaining. Each of these services includes prayers of confession, which ask for forgiveness for sins committed.

At the very end of the last service, the *shofar* is blown on more time; this time it is a long sustained blast signaling that Yom Kippur and its accompanying fast have ended. Many Jews will immediately head outside to hammer two pieces of wood together in preparation for the construction of a *sukkah,* a temporary wooden structure used in the celebration of *Sukkot* (the next holiday on the Jewish calendar).

All vows and oaths, all promises and obligations, and all renunciations and responses that we shall make from this Yom Kippur until the next—may it come to us in peace—all of them we retract. May we be absolved of them all, may we be released from them all, may they all be null and void, may they all be of no effect. May these vows not be vows, may these oaths not be oaths, may these responses not be responses.

KOL NIDRE PRAYER (ORIGIN UNKNOWN)

•

Depart (the synagogue) and eat your meal in joy.

THE TALMUD

Prior to the *Kol Nidre* service, the last meal for the next twenty-five hours is eaten. It is a traditional menu, but it is best to avoid salty or heavy foods that will make you sleepy and thirsty. Eat too lightly and you will feel dreadful the next day; it will be the last meal you eat for a full day. Many Jews complain of headaches from lack of food on Yom Kippur. In truth caffeine withdrawal likely yields the headache. While the menu depends on your personal tastes and preferences, a round *challah* is a must. Again the shape represents a smooth year with no bumps or edges.

After the last service, families often break their fasts at the synagogue with a piece of *challah* and some tea or sweet wine. Though many people are quite hungry at that point, a heavy meal does not seem terribly appealing, so it is traditional to dine on a dairy meal featuring fish, bagels, and light salads. Breaking the fast this way has become a tradition in American Jewish households; tuna, egg, whitefish and baked salmon salad, herring in cream sauce, spreads like flavored cream cheeses and *baba ghanouj*, and other dishes that can be made ahead of time are good choices. For those who prefer a hot dish, fruit or cheese blintzes, dairy kugel, and frittata are popular.

HOLIDAY CHALLAH

This recipe is a good choice for breaking the fast as well as for the last meal before the fast. It is fairly simple to follow even for the inexperienced bread maker.

    1 package dry yeast

    2 teaspoons granulated sugar

    1¼ cups lukewarm water

    4½ cups sifted all-purpose flour

    2 teaspoons salt

    2 eggs

    2 tablespoons oil

    1 egg yolk, beaten with 1 teaspoon water

Preheat oven to 375°F. Combine yeast, sugar, ¼ cup water, and let stand 5 minutes. Sift flour and salt into a large bowl. Make a well in the flour, and drop in the eggs, oil, water, and dissolved yeast mixture.

Mix well with your hands, turn out on a floured board and knead until your arms are tired, about 12 to 15 minutes. Cover, and let rise in a warm place for 1 hour.

Punch the dough down, allow it to recover, and let rise until doubled (if you poke your finger into it, the dent will spring back fairly quickly).

Divide dough in half and let rest for 10 minutes. Roll out each half into a long narrow cylindrical shape, like a fat snake. Coil each piece into a round shape on a nonstick cookie sheet.

Cover again and let rise until doubled in size. Brush with the beaten egg and water mixture and bake for 50 minutes.

Serves 10 to 12

MIDDLE EASTERN HUMMUS FOR BREAK-THE-FAST

One 18-ounce can chick-peas, drained
and rinsed

2 garlic cloves

½ teaspoon salt

½ cup tahini, mixed well

2 teaspoons freshly squeezed lemon juice

¼ cup olive oil, or to taste

2 tablespoons fresh parsley leaves, chopped

1 tablespoon pine nuts, toasted lightly
and coarsely chopped

In a food processor, purée the chick-peas with the garlic, salt, tahini, lemon juice, 3 tablespoons oil, and ¼ cup water, scraping down the sides between pulses, until the consistency is smooth. Add a bit more water, if necessary, to thin the hummus to the desired consistency and transfer the hummus to a bowl.

Wipe out the food processor. Add the parsley to the bowl and pulse parsley until puréed. Add the remaining oil to the parsley and pulse until the oil becomes bright green. Drizzle the oil over the hummus and sprinkle pine nuts on the top. Serve immediately.

Makes 3 cups

NOTE: The hummus may be made up to three days ahead if oil is added right before serving.

APRICOT CHICKEN

This recipe makes a lovely, not too heavy, but symbolically sweet dish for before the *Kol Nidre* service. Honey carrots, a traditional accompaniment to chicken, should be cut into disks, not sticks, to represent a round year without bumps or rough edges.

⅓ cup sliced almonds

½ cup apricot preserves

1½ tablespoons soy sauce

1 tablespoon whole-grain mustard

1 whole chicken, cut up into 8 pieces, and breasts cut in half

1½ teaspoon salt

½ teaspoon freshly ground black pepper

Preheat oven to 350°F. Toast almonds until golden, in a pie plate, in a toaster oven, or in the preheated oven for 8 to 10 minutes, shaking dish halfway through. Remove from oven and set aside.

Heat apricot preserves, soy sauce, and mustard in a small saucepan over low heat and stir until preserves have melted, then turn off heat.

Wash chicken, pat dry, and arrange chicken pieces in a large baking dish and season with salt and pepper. Pour sauce over chicken and bake until juices run clear, about 50 minutes. Baste halfway through with pan juices. Sprinkle with almond slices and serve immediately.

Serves 6

HONEY CARROTS

5 medium carrots peeled, trimmed, and cut into thin rounds

3 tablespoons honey

1 tablespoon finely chopped, peeled, fresh gingerroot

Salt and freshly ground pepper to taste

In a medium saucepan, cover carrots with cold water and bring to a boil. Simmer uncovered until tender, about 10 minutes.

Remove carrots from heat and drain but keep in pan. Pour honey and chopped ginger over hot carrots, stir well, and cover. Season with salt and pepper to taste and serve.

Serves 6

BEST CHEESE BLINTZES

This cheese blintzes recipe is sure to please. It comes from an old, food-stained, faded index card in my family's holiday recipe file. Once the blintzes have cooled, they can be frozen for up to six weeks. If you remove the blintzes from the freezer before heading to synagogue in the morning and put them in the fridge, they will be ready to eat after a few moments in the oven when you are ready to break your fast. You can heat them in a casserole dish briefly in a preheated oven, or even put them on a broiler pan and crisp them under the broiler for a few minutes before eating.

BLINTZES

½ cup all-purpose flour

Pinch salt

2 large eggs, well beaten

⅓ cup milk

1 tablespoon melted butter

1 tablespoon vegetable oil

FILLING

½ pound drained cottage cheese

2 egg yolks

¼ teaspoon ground cinnamon

1 tablespoon granulated sugar

1 tablespoon vegetable oil

TO MAKE THE BLINTZES: Sift dry ingredients together in a large bowl. Combine eggs, milk, and butter until smooth in a small bowl, gradually add to dry ingredients, stirring to remove lumps.

Grease a large griddle with vegetable oil and pour about 3 tablespoons of batter into pan. Tip pan to spread batter out completely. When batter begins to form blisters, gently remove and place on plate. Do not flip as with pancakes. Continue to make blintzes with the remaining batter. Stack the cooked blintzes on the plate.

TO MAKE THE FILLING: Place cheese in middle of cheesecloth or a clean kitchen towel. Twist ends to form a bag and squeeze out excess liquid. Pour into bowl and add remaining ingredients and mix well.

Remove one blintze from the stack, cooked side up onto a flat surface. Place a heaping tablespoon of filling in the center. Fold sides inward (like an envelope) and return to griddle, frying on all sides until golden brown. Add oil as needed. When the blintze starts to form blisters, gently remove it from the griddle with a spatula and place on a serving platter.

Continue the process until all the blintzes are filled and browned. Serve immediately, plain or with a topping.

Makes 12 blintzes

NOTE: Some people like a little sweet topping on their blintzes. Warmed berry preserves, applesauce, or simmered sliced apples with a teaspoon of sugar are good options.

STRAWBERRY SAUCE FOR BLINTZES

½ cup orange juice

⅓ cup honey

1 teaspoon pure vanilla extract

3 cups sliced hulled strawberries

Simmer orange juice and honey in heavy medium skillet over medium heat until reduced by half, about 4 minutes. Transfer to large bowl. Stir in vanilla and strawberries. Cover with plastic wrap and refrigerate until cool. Spoon over warm blintzes and serve.

Makes 3 cups

BLUEBERRY SAUCE FOR BLINTZES

5 cups frozen unsweetened blueberries

½ cup granulated sugar

1 teaspoon grated lemon zest

1½ tablespoons cornstarch

Freshly squeezed lemon juice (optional),
to taste

Combine blueberries, sugar, and lemon zest in large bowl. Let stand at room temperature until berries defrost and sugar dissolves, about 1½ hours. Stir mixture occasionally. The berries and sugar should be a liquid consistency.

Strain blueberry mixture thoroughly, reserving juices. Place cornstarch in heavy medium saucepan. Gradually add reserved juices to cornstarch, whisking until smooth. Whisk over high heat until syrup boils and is thick and clear, about 2 minutes. Transfer to bowl. Cool 15 minutes. Add blueberry mixture to syrup, and stir thoroughly. Taste and adjust tartness with lemon juice. Spoon over blintzes and serve.

Makes 5 cups

VEGETABLE KUGEL

Another nice choice for breaking the fast is a vegetable kugel. Often served on Passover and made with matzohs, this kugel is lighter and won't weigh you down. Many kugels are made with cottage cheese or raisins. I've chosen a vegetable recipe that reheats well and makes a great post-holiday breakfast or lunch.

5 cups egg noodles

½ teaspoon cumin

½ teaspoon sage

½ teaspoon oregano

2 cups grated carrots

2 cups grated zucchini

8 ounces sliced button mushrooms

1 cup grated onion

2 tablespoons balsamic vinegar

4 tablespoons margarine (melted)

5 large eggs, lightly beaten

Salt and pepper to taste

Preheat oven to 375°F. Boil noodles according to package directions. Drain and set aside. Put all spices in a large bowl and add carrots and zucchini and set aside.

In a large skillet, sauté mushrooms and onions with vinegar over medium heat until the liquid is reduced, about 5 minutes. Add to spices, carrots, and zucchini mixture, and then pour in noodles. Mix well, and then add margarine and eggs. Thoroughly mix again.

Lightly grease a 9- by 13-inch glass baking dish and pour in batter. Bake for about 20 minutes (25 minutes for a well-done kugel). Serve immediately. This dish may be reheated if stored tightly covered and chilled.

Serves 12 to 14

DAYENU
(A TRADITIONAL PASSOVER SONG)

ILU HO-TSI, HO-TSI-ONU,
HO-TSI-ONU MI-MITZ-RA-YIM
HO-TSI-ONU MI-MITZ-RA-YIM
DA-YE-NU

CHORUS
DA-DA-YE-NU,
DA-DA-YE-NU,
DA-DA-YE-NU,
DA-YE-NU,
DA-YE-NU,
(REPEAT)

ILU NA-TAN, NA-TAN-LA-NU,
NA-TAN-LA-NU TO-RAT E-MET,
TO-RAT E-MET NA-TAN-LA-NU,
DA-YE-NU
(REPEAT)

CHORUS

TRANSLATION:
IF MORNING WILL COME AND DISCOVER US
IF THE HEART WILL FILL UP AGAIN, IT IS ENOUGH FOR US
IF, IN THE WARM SUN, WHEAT FIELDS WILL RIPEN
IF WE BREAK OUR HUNGER AND THIRST

IT IS ENOUGH FOR US
AND IF A BIT OF COMPASSION STILL REMAINS
AND WE HAVE A REASON TO BE HAPPY
IT IS ENOUGH FOR US

Chanukah

Celebrate with gladness like the 'Feast of Tabernacles the resurrection of the temple, remembering how, not long before, during the 'Feast of 'Tabernacles, they had been wandering like wild beasts in the mountains and the caves.

THE BIBLE

The next holiday on the Jewish calendar is Chanukah, the "Festival of Lights." This post-biblical holiday marks the victory of the Maccabees, a band of Jewish freedom fighters who prevailed over their oppressors in the second century. The word Chanukah means dedication. The holiday commemorates the rededication of the temple after years of defilement and pagan worship. The tradition of lighting candles for eight nights recalls the miracle of a small vial of oil intended to light the synagogue for one night lasting for eight nights instead. This miraculous event provided the Maccabees with enough time to prepare sanctified oil with which to light the synagogue.

Since this is a post-biblical holiday, there are no rules in the Torah or other sacred texts as to how the holiday should be observed. While it is a minor holiday, Chanukah has grown in importance most likely because it falls around the Christmas season and gives Jews an opportunity to exchange gifts and gather for festive parties.

Though my family does exchange gifts, I have never strung lights or otherwise decorated except with a *menorah*. To have a Christmas tree or lights hanging on your eaves or even a wreath on the front door, as a Jew, regardless of whom your descendants are, seems a bit too assimilated for my tastes. If you are compelled to illuminate something, help a non-Jewish friend decorate their tree as we do each year so as to enjoy the festive feeling of the season without compromising your own values. There is no such thing as a Chanukah bush in Jewish law!

A great miracle happened here.
SYMBOLIC MEANING ON A DREIDEL

•

Blessed are you eternal God who worked miracles for our ancestors in ancient days at this time of year.
TRADITIONAL PRAYER

Chanukkiah

A special candelabrum known as a *menorah* (or a *chanukkiah*) is used for the candle lighting. Technically, the seven-candle *menorah* is the national symbol of Israel; for the "Festival of Lights" an eight-candle *chanukkiah* is used. This candelabrum has an additional space for another candle called the *shamash*, which is lit first and used to light all the others from right to left. An additional candle is lit on each successive night.

Mention the dead on the Day of Atonement and donate to charity in their memory.

ANCIENT JEWISH TEXT

Thou dost reach out Thy hand
to transgressors; Thy right hand
is extended to receive repentant sinners.

THE BIBLE

•

Celebrate with gladness like the Feast of
Tabernacles the resurrection of the
temple, remembering how, not long
before, during the Feast of Tabernacles,
they had been wandering like wild beasts
in the mountains and the caves.

THE BIBLE

ROCK OF AGES

Rock of Ages, let our song
Praise Thy saving power;
Thou, amidst the raging foes,
Wast our sheltering tower.
Furious they assailed us,
But Thine arm availed us,
And Thy Word
Broke their sword
When our own strength failed us.

Kindling new the holy lamps,
Priests, approved in suffering,
Purified the nation's shrine,
Brought to God their offering.
And His courts surrounding
Hear, in joy abounding,
Happy throngs,
Singing songs
With a mighty sounding.

CHILDREN OF THE MARTYR RACE,
WHETHER FREE OR FETTERED,
WAKE THE ECHOES OF THE SONGS
WHERE YE MAY BE SCATTERED.
YOURS THE MESSAGE CHEERING
THAT THE TIME IS NEARING
WHICH WILL SEE
ALL MEN FREE,
TYRANTS DISAPPEARING.

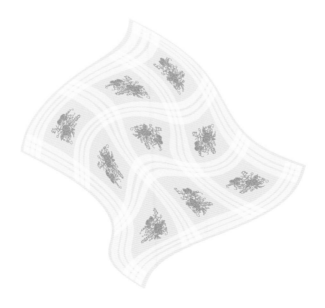

O CHANUKAH

O Chanukah O Chanukah,
Come light the menorah

Let's have a party, we'll all dance the hora

Gather round the table, we'll give you a treat

Dreidels to play with and latkes to eat

And while we are playing,
the candles are burning low

One for each night, they shed a sweet light
to remind us of days long ago
(repeat)

MY DREIDEL

I HAVE A LITTLE DREIDEL,
I MADE IT OUT OF CLAY,
AND WHEN IT'S DRY AND READY
THEN DREIDEL I SHALL PLAY!
OH DREIDEL, DREIDEL, DREIDEL
I MADE IT OUT OF CLAY
OH DREIDEL, DREIDEL, DREIDEL
NOW DREIDEL I SHALL PLAY

IT HAS A LOVELY BODY
WITH A LEG SO SHORT AND THIN
AND WHEN IT GETS ALL TIRED
IT DROPS AND THEN I WIN!

OH DREIDEL, DREIDEL, DREIDEL,
WITH A LEG SO SHORT AND THIN,
OH DREIDEL, DREIDEL, DREIDEL,
IT DROPS AND THEN I WIN.

Jews are not required to go to synagogue during this eight-day period. Instead, many families choose to have parties, sharing potato pancakes (latkes), eating jelly-filled donuts (*sufganiyot*), and other treats fried in oil. Entertainment centers around the spinning of the *dreidel*, a four-sided top with Hebrew letters on each side. Each participant starts with a small pile of nuts, raisins, or other small items. Everyone antes up and the *dreidel* is spun. Depending on how it lands, the spinner wins and collects the pot, has to ante up again, takes half the pot or the game continues. My family uses chocolate chips as the ante to sweeten the pot. What a lovely way to pass the time waiting for the latkes to cook!

The traditional observance of this "Festival of Lights" should include latkes. In our house, the smells coming from my cooktop exhaust hood inevitably draw a sigh from my non-Jewish neighbor. "It must be a holiday, because I can't resist the smells coming from your house," I am told. What could be better than onions and potatoes fried in oil to a golden brown and well salted! When my children were younger, my dear friends, Nancy and Maud, neither of whom are Jewish, would always manage to schedule our weekly playgroup at my home right around Chanukah and plead with me for latkes. Even now, they hint around just as the holiday is starting that they are free to pop by for a few latkes.

In the recent past, creative chefs have tweaked the notion of a pancake made exclusively from potatoes. A quick search yields recipes for root vegetable pancakes, carrot and zucchini pancakes, and just about any other vegetable that can be julienned and fried. Still other recipes offer a low-fat alternative to latkes; baking them may cut the fat, but it also cuts the flavor. Better to eat fewer fried latkes than many baked ones! Like matzoh balls, there are many different opinions on what makes the best latkes. Some prefer lacy, thin ones that crunch when bitten; others swear by thicker ones with a softer texture. Whatever your preference, the secret to the most delicious latkes is to continuously drain the potatoes to prevent them from becoming soggy and only flip once. Serve them with homemade applesauce.

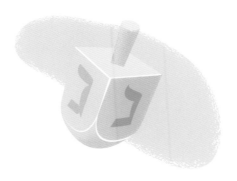

POTATO LATKES

6 medium baking potatoes, peeled

¼ teaspoon baking powder

1 medium onion

2 medium eggs, lightly beaten

2 tablespoons all-purpose flour

1 cup vegetable oil

Grate the potatoes in a food processor fitted with a grating disk. Put the grated potatoes into a large bowl and sprinkle with the baking powder to keep them from turning brown. Grate the onion and add to the potatoes.

Using a saucer slightly smaller than the bowl, press down on the potatoes and pour out the excess liquid. Press and drain again. Add the beaten eggs and flour and mix well with clean hands.

Heat oil over medium-high heat in a large heavy skillet. With clean hands, take about a tablespoon's worth of the mixture and squeeze out the excess liquid. Carefully drop into the hot oil, pressing down with the back of a spoon to flatten.

Cook for about 4 minutes or until edges begin to brown. Turn only once and cook for another 3 to 4 minutes.

Transfer each latke to a platter lined with paper towels and continue to cook them until all the batter is gone. Liberally salt the latkes and serve immediately.

Makes about 25 small or 18 large latkes

HOMEMADE APPLESAUCE

10 Macintosh or Granny Smith apples

¾ cup water

1 to 2 teaspoons granulated sugar

Peel, core, and seed apples. Place in large saucepan with water and bring to a boil. Reduce heat, cover, and allow to simmer about 20 to 25 minutes or until apples are falling apart.

Remove from heat and press down with a potato masher to remove any lumps. Sweeten with sugar to taste and serve.

Makes 5 cups

NOTE: The applesauce may be stored for up to a week in a sealed container in the refrigerator.

RASPBERRY APPLESAUCE

1 cup raspberries

¼ cup water

¼ cup packed brown sugar

⅓ cup frozen apple juice concentrate undiluted, thawed

1 tablespoon freshly squeezed lemon juice

5 whole cloves

1 cinnamon stick

5 cups Granny Smith (or other tart) apples, cored, peeled, and grated

Boil raspberries in water for 2 minutes, then mash, strain, and discard the seeds. Set aside. Mix sugar, juices, cloves, and cinnamon in a saucepan and boil over medium heat. Reduce the heat and simmer uncovered for 3 minutes. Add apples and simmer for 30 minutes, or until tender. Remove from heat and discard the whole spices. Stir in the raspberry purée. Mash the apples to a desired consistency. Cool and serve over latkes.

Makes 4 cups

Passover

*How is this night different from
all other nights?*

*On other nights we eat leavened or
unleavened bread; on this night why only
unleavened bread?*

*On all other nights we eat all kinds
of herbs; on this night why only
bitter herbs?*

*On other nights we do not dip herbs even
once; on this night, why do we dip twice?*

*On other nights we eat upright or
leaning; why tonight do we all lean?*

Passover, a major holiday celebrated in the spring, is observed for a week, and starts on the 15th day of *Nisan* (usually during April). For non-Jews, the appearance of matzoh and macaroons at the grocery store is a sure sign that the holiday is afoot.

Like most children raised in an observant Jewish home, my memories of Passover includes the hunt for the *afikoman*, hearing about a plague of locusts, and eating jelly sandwiches on matzoh for a week. My mother's parents were Orthodox Jews who kept a kosher home, and I recall hearing stories of many sets of dishes and ritual *chametz* (leavened products) hunts. To get ready for this food-intensive holiday, I find myself engaged in "competitive" Passover buying the week before the holiday starts, and search high and low for those desirable Passover foods; schmaltz (rendered chicken fat), chocolate-covered matzohs, and chocolate-chip macaroons. I put my own personal spin on the *chametz* hunt by relining all my kitchen shelves and cabinets, and hiding the leavened products I don't toss out behind a makeshift cardboard "wall" in my pantry.

The holiday has its origins in the celebration of the Israelites' liberation from their enslavement in Egypt and the tyranny of the Pharaohs. There is more to the story however. The Pharaoh had decreed that all firstborn Jewish sons were to be put to death. Moses' life was spared when his mother placed him in a basket in the river. He was found by the Pharaoh's daughter. She raised him as her own and his true identity was concealed for a time. As an adult, Moses witnessed a Jewish slave being beaten by an overseer. Moses killed the overseer and was sentenced to death by the Pharaoh and so had to flee Egypt. It is said that God summoned Moses back to Egypt to free the Hebrew slaves.

When the Pharaoh turned Moses down after he requested freedom for the Jews, God cast ten plagues upon the Egyptians; these included locusts, frogs, lice, cattle disease, hail, and other nastiness. The worst of the plagues was the certain death of firstborn Egyptian boys, much like the decree the Pharaoh had once handed down against Hebrew boys. The name Passover refers to the symbolic lamb's blood smeared on Jewish doors to indicate that the house should be "passed over" by the decree and any firstborn male child within be spared death.

The Pharaoh panicked and announced that the slaves would indeed be freed. In their haste to leave before anyone else had a change of heart, the Hebrews had no time to allow their bread to rise and so traveled with unrisen bread, or matzoh.

We honor and memorialize their speedy departure by eating unleavened bread for the days of Passover, and ridding our homes of *chametz*.

To offer up the meal offering of the Omer
on the morrow after the first day of
Passover, together with one lamb. Not to
eat bread made of new grain before the
Omer of barley has been offered up on the
second day of Passover.

BIBLICAL COMMANDMENT

They shall take some of the blood and put it on the two doorposts and the lintel of the houses in which they are to eat it. The blood on the houses shall be a sign for you; when I see the blood I will pass over you, so that no plague will destroy you when I strike the land of Egypt.

EXODUS

•

Come therefore, I will send you to Pharaoh and you will free my people, the Israelites, from Egypt.

EXODUS

Many Jews use this holiday as an opportunity to do a spring cleaning of the kitchen. More observant Jews will search with a candle and a feather the day before the holiday begins and sweep out any last traces of leavening. Kosher restaurants often close for the week rather than try to assure their premises are completely devoid of *chametz*. Many Jews will also put away all cookware, dishes, and cutlery used for the other fifty-one weeks of the year and take out their dedicated Passover items. This way, there is no confusion about what may contain traces of *chametz*.

What exactly is *chametz*? Well, the definition is clear but the extent to which you take your avoidance of *chametz* is dependent on your level of observance. Many Reform Jews choose to not eat bread during the week and might even skip their morning bowl of cornflakes. *Chametz* really means wheat, barley, rye, spelt, or oats. Ashkenazi rabbis have said *kiniot* (rice), millet, corn, or legumes such as soybeans and lentils, are also off limits. More observant Jews will rid their homes of everything that might contain one of these ingredients or a derivative of them. For example, soda pop has corn syrup as do many other foods and drinks, so if you are making a genuine attempt to rid your diet of these items for the week, be prepared to read a lot of ingredient lists. Most large grocers will carry some of the items you would need to survive a week without *chametz*; these include Passover cakes, crackers, cereal, chocolate drink mix, soups, and drinks. Many food manufacturers will even produce "kosher for Passover" versions of their usual products for the week. Otherwise, prepare to do a good deal of cooking because the best way to make sure it's "kosher for Passover" is to make it yourself.

You shall eat nothing leavened; in all your settlements shall you eat matzoh.

EXODUS

●

And thou shalt tell thy son in that day, saying: It is because of that which the Lord did for me when I came forth out of Egypt.

EXODUS

*Seven days you shall eat
unleavened bread.*
EXODUS

•

*The sacrifice of the Paschal lamb is the
Passover sacrifice to the Lord because he
passed over the houses of the Israelites in
Egypt when he smote the Egyptians.*
EXODUS

Had Gadya

ONE LITTLE GOAT, ONE LITTLE GOAT,
MY FATHER BOUGHT FOR TWO ZUZIM.
ONE LITTLE GOAT, ONE LITTLE GOAT.

THEN CAME A CAT AND ATE THE GOAT
MY FATHER BOUGHT FOR TWO ZUZIM.
ONE LITTLE GOAT, ONE LITTLE GOAT.

THEN CAME A DOG AND BIT THE CAT,
THAT ATE THE GOAT
MY FATHER BOUGHT FOR TWO ZUZIM.
ONE LITTLE GOAT, ONE LITTLE GOAT.

THEN CAME A STICK AND BEAT THE DOG,
THAT BIT THE CAT
THAT ATE THE GOAT MY FATHER BOUGHT FOR
TWO ZUZIM.
ONE LITTLE GOAT, ONE LITTLE GOAT.

THEN CAME A FIRE AND BURNED THE STICK
THAT BEAT THE DOG
THAT BIT THE CAT
THAT ATE THE GOAT
MY FATHER BOUGHT FOR TWO ZUZIM.
ONE LITTLE GOAT, ONE LITTLE GOAT.

THEN CAME THE WATER AND QUENCHED THE FIRE,
THAT BURNED THE STICK
THAT BEAT THE DOG
THAT BIT THE CAT
THAT ATE THE GOAT
MY FATHER BOUGHT FOR TWO ZUZIM.
ONE LITTLE GOAT, ONE LITTLE GOAT.

THEN CAME AN OX AND DRANK THE WATER,
THAT QUENCHED THE FIRE
THAT BURNED THE STICK
THAT BEAT THE DOG
THAT BIT THE CAT
THAT ATE THE GOAT
MY FATHER BOUGHT FOR TWO ZUZIM.
ONE LITTLE GOAT, ONE LITTLE GOAT.

THEN CAME A SHOHET AND SLAUGHTERED THE OX,
THAT DRANK THE WATER THAT QUENCHED THE FIRE
THAT BURNED THE STICK THAT BEAT THE DOG
THAT BIT THE CAT THAT ATE THE GOAT
MY FATHER BOUGHT FOR TWO ZUZIM.
ONE LITTLE GOAT, ONE LITTLE GOAT.

continued...

THEN CAME THE ANGEL OF DEATH AND
KILLED THE SHOHET,
THAT SLAUGHTERED THE OX THAT DRANK THE WATER
THAT QUENCHED THE FIRE THAT BURNED THE STICK
THAT BEAT THE DOG THAT BIT THE CAT
THAT ATE THE GOAT
MY FATHER BOUGHT FOR TWO ZUZIM.
ONE LITTLE GOAT, ONE LITTLE GOAT.

THEN CAME THE HOLY ONE, BLESSED BE HE,
AND SLEW THE ANGEL OF DEATH,
THAT KILLED THE SHOHET THAT SLAUGHTERED THE OX
THAT DRANK THE WATER THAT QUENCHED THE FIRE
THAT BURNED THE STICK THAT BEAT THE DOG
THAT BIT THE CAT THAT ATE THE GOAT
MY FATHER BOUGHT FOR TWO ZUZIM.
ONE LITTLE GOAT, ONE LITTLE GOAT.

Blessed are you, our eternal God,
Ruler of the Universe, who has
sanctified us by Your commandments
and enjoined us to remove leavened food
from our homes.

PASSOVER PRAYER

•

All chametz in my possession which I
have not seen or removed, or of which I
am not aware, is hereby nullified and
ownerless as the dust of the earth.

PASSOVER PRAYER

Another reason for the observance of Passover is the celebration of the first period of freedom for the Israelites. Many of 618 *Mitzvot* state how we should observe Passover. Since the holiday also commemorates the first harvest, many of the Commandments instruct us in how to honor God with offerings from the harvest. The reference to the Paschal (Passover) lamb is that which was sacrificed and roasted the night before the plague of the firstborn was passed down. It supplied the blood to be painted on the doors of the Israelites. Here are the Passover *Mitzvot*:

* To observe the second Passover

* To eat the flesh of the Paschal lamb on it, with unleavened bread and bitter herbs

* Not to leave any flesh of the Paschal lamb brought on the second Passover until the morning

* Not to break a bone of the Paschal lamb brought on the second Passover

* To slay the Paschal lamb

* To eat the flesh of the Paschal sacrifice on the night of the fifteenth of *Nisan*

* Not to eat the flesh of the Paschal lamb raw or sodden

* Not to leave any portion of the flesh of the Paschal sacrifice until the morning unconsumed

* Not to give the flesh of the Paschal lamb to an Israelite who had become an apostate

* Not to give flesh of the Paschal lamb to a stranger who lives among you to eat

* Not to take any of the flesh of the Paschal lamb from the company's place of assembly

* Not to break a bone of the Paschal lamb

* That the uncircumcised shall not eat of the flesh of the Paschal lamb

* Not to slaughter the Paschal lamb while there is *chametz* in the home

Traditionally, all observant Jews will gather with family and friends to celebrate Passover with a Seder, a festive holiday service and meal, on the first night and possibly for a second the next night. The Seder is held because Jewish parents have the obligation to teach their children about the hard-won freedom of the Israelites.

I host at least one Seder each Passover and can safely say that it is the most exhausting holiday to celebrate in your home. There are endless small details to attend to, not least of which is making sure that despite the absence of leavening, the food is delicious. I prefer a menu with a mix of traditional and modern dishes. A creative *charoses* (matzoh spread), a lighter vegetable dish, and a flourless chocolate cake can bring your Seder into the 21st century without compromising respect for tradition.

The Seder should include several elements. Today, the service remains essentially as it has been for thousands of years, with a few additions to acknowledge the role of women. On Passover many things are done differently than on other Jewish holidays: The *Mishnah*, a sacred text, tells us that even the poorest man in Israel must recline while eating on the first night of Passover. Long ago, free men would normally recline at meals and on this night all must demonstrate that they are not enslaved. At some point in history, the tradition of reclining while eating disappeared, but it is required at the Seder. Seder guests must drink four cups of wine during the course of the service. A Seder plate must be on the table and contain several items: three sheets of matzoh, piled one on top of another; a roasted egg; a roasted lamb shank bone (a reminder of the sacrifice of the Paschal lamb); a dish of salt water (a symbol of the Israelites' tears); maror (any bitter herb like horseradish); and charoses (a spread made from almonds, apples, and wine and symbolic of the mortar the Israelites used to build the Pharaoh's structures when enslaved).

My family's Seders usually start with the best of intentions. Cousin Arnie, the only one at our Seder who can chant the prayers in Hebrew with the proper gravitas, washes his hands and begins. Given the growing number of children present and the pleasure of family brought together on a joyous occasion, a general atmosphere of frivolity and laughter takes over. The four questions are passed from child to child each year as learning to read both English and Hebrew is accomplished. Every Seder is ended no matter who is present with a rousing rendition of Dayenu, a traditional Passover song, and the inevitable question, "What is a zuzim anyway?" It was a coin in biblical times.

The traditional Seder service should include the following steps in order:

KADDESH, OR SANCTIFICATION

REHAZ (WASH): Usually, the leader of the Seder washes his hands in a ritual of purification.

KARPAS (GREENS): the parsley is dipped in salt water

YAHAZ (DIVISION): the middle matzoh is broken in two and one half is hidden. This hidden portion is known as the *afikoman* (the after-meal) and is eaten at the end of the meal, after it is found by the children in attendance. A prize is usually given to the finder. Make sure whomever hides the matzoh picks a spot not adjacent to Grandma's family heirloom figurines.

MAROR: the bitter herbs are dipped in the *charoses* and eaten.

KOREKH (BINDING): a sandwich is made of pieces of the bottom matzoh and bitter herbs and eaten.

SHULHAN ARUKH (PREPARED TABLE): the festive meal is eaten.

ZAFUN (HIDDEN): the afikoman is found and eaten.

Elijah's Cup

One more tradition that many families include is the placement of a full cup of wine in a *Kiddush* cup on the table. This is Elijah's cup. Elijah, believed to herald the arrival of the Messiah, is welcomed to the table toward the end of the Seder by opening a nearby door or window. Some more modern families might also include a Miriam's cup, acknowledging the role of women in Jewish history.

THE PASSOVER MEAL

A common complaint among Jews celebrating Passover is that the food can really weigh them down. Eating heavy dishes like brisket and those made with matzoh meal for eight days can mess with one's digestive system. In the past, it was expected that a few extra pounds would probably appear during the holiday, but recently, creative recipe development, some thoughtful chefs, and an eye on fresh ingredients has yielded a new Passover cuisine that is lighter, tastier, and less likely to weigh one down. Here are a few more modern recipes that Passover observers will enjoy, as well as some classic dishes for the Seder table. Recipes for other holidays in this book can be used for Passover as long as they contain no *chametz*. Two favorites are the chicken soup with matzoh balls and the brisket from the *Shabbat* recipes. It's great to serve the same foods your *Bubbe* (grandma) made, but offering Seder guests a few new choices is just as nice!

GRAMMY'S MATZOH KUGEL

8 medium eggs, separated

½ cup granulated sugar

5 apples, peeled, cored, and grated

½ cup matzoh meal

1 teaspoon grated lemon zest

Handful chopped almonds

Preheat oven to 325°F. Lightly grease a springform baking pan. Beat egg whites until they form stiff peaks and set aside. Stir the sugar and egg yolks together well in a large bowl, add grated apple, and mix well. Stir in matzoh meal and lemon zest. Fold in egg whites and pour into baking pan.

Bake for about 1 hour, or until top is lightly browned and kugel is firm to the touch.

Sprinkle with chopped almonds, slice into wedges, and serve warm.

Serves 10

CLASSIC ASHKENAZIC CHAROSES

2 Granny Smith or other tart apples, peeled and coarsely chopped

1 cup coarsely chopped almonds or walnuts

1 teaspoon ground cinnamon

2 teaspoons honey

4 tablespoons kosher sweet wine, such as Manischewitz Concord Grape

Place all ingredients in a food processor fitted with a steel blade. Pulse for a second at a time until well-mixed and pasty but not puréed. Sweeten with additional wine or sugar if needed.

Makes enough for 12 matzoh sandwiches for two Seders

NOTE: This dish may be made ahead and stored in a sealed container in the refrigerator.

SEPHARDIC CHAROSES

For our Seders we like to experiment a little and try a new *charoses* (matzoh spread) each year in addition to the traditional apples and almonds mixture. Passover foods should remind us of what we might have eaten had we been forced to flee on short notice so long ago, and not be so devoid of the familiar matzoh ingredient that it's as if it wasn't a holiday at all.

1 cup chopped, pitted dates

½ cup raisins & ¾ cup almonds

½ cup kosher sweet wine

2 tangerines, seeded, and coarsely chopped

½ cup honey

½ teaspoon ground cinnamon

½ cup pine nuts

Pulse dates, raisins, almonds, wine, tangerine, honey, cinnamon, and pine nuts in food processor until mixture resembles a coarse paste. If consistency is too sticky, add wine by the tablespoon.

Makes enough for 12 matzoh sandwiches for two Seders

ORANGE CHICKEN

1 whole chicken, cut up, breasts halved

1 cup orange juice

1 cup white wine

1 medium onion, sliced thinly

1 stalk celery with greens attached, chopped

¼ cup raisins

3 tablespoons vegetable oil

1 tablespoon grated orange zest

1 teaspoon cumin

1 teaspoon paprika

1 orange, peeled, and thinly sliced for garnish

Place all ingredients except orange slices and chicken in a large bowl and stir well. Arrange chicken in a large casserole dish so that no pieces overlap. Pour marinade over chicken, making sure that each piece is coated. Tip dish, and with a soup ladle, spoon marinade over chicken again. Cover and chill overnight or at least for 3 hours.

Preheat oven to 350°F. Bake for 1 hour or until juices run clear.

Remove from oven and place chicken pieces on a platter. Pour remaining liquid into a medium saucepan and cook over high heat for 2 to 3 minutes or until slightly thickened. Pour over chicken, garnish with orange slices, and serve.

Serves 6 to 8

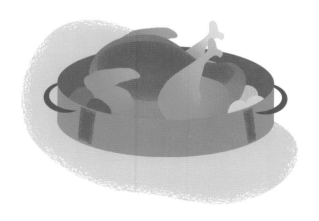

PASSOVER ASPARAGUS TART

1 tablespoon vegetable oil

1 pound medium asparagus spears, trimmed, and cut into 1-inch pieces

2 tablespoons olive oil

1 medium onion, diced

5 pieces matzoh (plain or egg)

6 large eggs, well beaten

1 teaspoon fresh tarragon, chopped

1 teaspoon kosher salt

½ teaspoon ground white pepper

Preheat oven to 350°F. Grease a 9- by 13-inch glass dish with the vegetable oil. Set aside.

Bring a small saucepan of 5 cups of cold, lightly salted water to boil. Add asparagus and simmer for 3 minutes. Remove from heat, and with a slotted spoon, remove asparagus and set aside. Keep the hot water for softening the matzoh.

Heat the olive oil in a medium skillet over medium heat. Add onion and cook until soft, about 4 minutes. Remove from heat and set aside. Crumble matzoh into a bowl and cover with the hot water from the asparagus and set aside for 5 minutes. Drain matzoh and pour in beaten eggs, asparagus, onion, tarragon, salt, and pepper.

Pour batter into prepared pan and bake for 30 minutes, or until puffy and lightly browned on top. Slice into wedges and serve immediately.

Serves 12

SINFUL CARAMEL CHOCOLATE MATZOHS

4 to 6 matzoh sheets (plain or egg)

2 sticks unsalted butter (or unsalted margarine)

1 cup firmly packed brown sugar

¾ cup semisweet chocolate chips

Preheat the oven to 350°F. Line a large cookie sheet with foil, and place a sheet of parchment paper on top of the foil. Place matzohs on the cookie sheet, breaking pieces as needed to fill in spaces.

In a large heavy saucepan, mix the butter and the brown sugar. Cook over medium heat, stirring constantly, until mixture comes to a boil. Boil for 3 minutes, stirring so it doesn't burn. Remove from heat and pour over the matzohs, covering completely. If mixture is sticky, use the back of a lightly greased spoon to smooth it out.

Place entire cookie sheet into the freezer and chill until firm, about 1 hour. Break into small pieces and serve. The matzohs may be kept in a resealable container for up to a week. Store in cool place.

Makes 24 to 30 pieces

PASSOVER ALMOND TORTE

8 medium eggs, separated

1½ cups granulated sugar

1½ cups almonds, unblanched and coarsely chopped

¾ cup matzoh cake meal

1 teaspoon ground cinnamon

1 teaspoon pure vanilla extract

Freshly squeezed lemon juice to taste

Preheat oven to 325°F. Separate egg whites from yolks. Beat yolks, add sugar, and continue to beat until thickened. Add the rest of the ingredients. Beat egg whites until they form stiff peaks. Fold into yolk and almond mixture, carefully mixing well. Pour into ungreased springform baking pan and bake for about 1 hour or until golden and crust is firm.

Serves 10

FRUIT COMPOTE

3 cups fresh Bing cherries, cut into
¼-inch dice

½ cup diced fresh pineapple

½ mango, cut into ¼-inch dice

2 firm-ripe apricots, peeled and diced

½ cup raspberries, picked over and quartered

1 teaspoon granulated sugar

In a medium size bowl, gently toss compote ingredients together. Let stand 15 minutes.

Makes 5 cups

CHOCOLATE COCONUT MACAROONS

1⅓ cups (about 8 ounces)
mini semisweet chocolate chips

2 large egg whites

¼ teaspoon salt

½ cup granulated sugar

½ teaspoon pure vanilla extract

1½ cups sweetened flaked coconut

Preheat oven to 325°F. Line 2 large rimmed baking sheets with parchment paper.

Place 1 cup of the chocolate chips in microwave-safe bowl. Microwave on low setting at 10-second intervals until chocolate is melted, stirring to avoid sticking. Cool to room temperature. Using electric mixer, beat egg whites and salt in medium bowl until soft peaks form. Gradually add sugar, then vanilla, beating until whites are thick and glossy. Fold in melted chocolate and coconut, then remaining ⅓ cup chocolate chips.

Drop batter by heaping teaspoonfuls onto prepared sheets, spacing ⅓ inches apart. Bake for 10 minutes. Switch lower tray with upper tray. Bake until tops are dry and cracked and tester inserted into centers comes out with moist crumbs attached, about 10 minutes longer. Cool cookies on sheets on racks. Store airtight at room temperature for up to 2 days.

Makes 24 cookies

VARIATIONS: For Chocolate Almond Macaroons, replace coconut with ½ cup finely chopped almonds. For Orange-scented Chocolate Macaroons, replace coconut with 2 tablespoons grated orange zest.

Shavuot

Shavuot commemorates when Moses, after fleeing the Pharaoh in Egypt and spending seven weeks in the desert, first received the Ten Commandments and the Torah from God at the foot of Mt. Sinai. It also marks the end of the first harvest. In biblical times a sacrifice of the first cut wheat was required. This holiday usually falls in early to mid-June and occurs precisely fifty days after the second day of Passover. The most important rite of the holiday is the observance of *tikkun,* (an all-night gathering for prayer). Jews will come together at their synagogue or in a home for prayer and all-night study.

The celebration of Confirmation, (a reaffirmation of one's commitment to Judaism) also takes place on *Shavuot.* I chose to continue my religious education after I celebrated my *Bat Mitzvah* by being confirmed. I was called to the Torah in June of my 16th year. Presented with a copy of the Bible, I and twenty-five others acknowledged our commitment to the Commandments on the same day the Israelites confirmed their faith at Mt. Sinai. As most thirteen-year-olds, myself included, are really too immature to grasp the significance of their *Bar* or *Bat Mitzvah*, and perhaps have a hard time looking past the inevitable party, a reexamination of one's commitment to Judaism a few years later seems appropriate. It is wholly a Reform and Conservative ritual; few if any Orthodox Jews celebrate *Shavuot* in this way.

Many observant Jews will eat only dairy on this holiday. This tradition may come from knowing, after receiving the Torah, that certain meat was not kosher, and so only dairy is consumed. This may or may not be accurate, but the tradition has stuck.

And all His desire is that
His chosen people
Will study His Torah and pray to Him,
For they are inscribed in His tefillin,
"Who is like Your people, Israel,
One nation in the world!"
AKDAMUT (TRADITIONAL SHAVUOT PRAYER)

•

To bring on Shavuot loaves of bread
together with the sacrifices which are
then offered up in connection with
the loaves.
BIBLICAL COMMANDMENT

WHOLE BAKED SALMON WITH CUCUMBER DILL SAUCE

One 4-pound whole salmon with head and tail, scaled and carefully split

6 scallions, chopped

5 tablespoons freshly squeezed lemon juice

2 tablespoons olive oil

½ cup dry white wine

Salt and freshly ground pepper to taste

Paper-thin cucumber slices, lemon wedges, and fresh dill sprigs as garnish

CUCUMBER DILL SAUCE

1 cup coarsely chopped fresh dill

¾ cup Kirby or English cucumber, peeled and coarsely chopped

½ cup mayonnaise

½ cup low-fat sour cream

Salt and freshly ground pepper to taste

Preheat oven to 325°F. Place two heavy aluminum foil sheets on a large baking sheet. Place fish on foil. Sprinkle half of the scallions and half of the lemon juice inside fish. Drizzle remaining lemon juice and oil over the salmon. Pour wine over fish and sprinkle with salt and pepper. Scatter remaining scallions around fish. Fold foil, sealing the salmon tightly but leaving airspace between the fish and foil. Bake for 1 hour.

Remove fish from oven. Open foil and let fish cool for 1 hour. Reseal foil and refrigerate until cold, about 4 hours.

Open foil. Carefully remove skin from fish. Scrape off any gray flesh. Transfer fish to platter.

TO MAKE CUCUMBER DILL SAUCE: Blend dill and cucumber in processor until cucumber is finely chopped; transfer to medium bowl. Whisk in mayonnaise and sour cream. Season with salt and pepper. Cover with plastic wrap and refrigerate until ready to serve.

Serve Cucumber Dill Sauce in a bowl placed next to the salmon. Garnish top of fish with cucumber slices. Surround with lemon wedges and dill sprigs.

Serves 8

NOTE: The salmon can be prepared one day ahead. Keep refrigerated until ready to serve.

HORSERADISH CREAM

This recipe provides a lively alternative to a traditional Cucumber Dill Sauce.

¼ cup low-fat sour cream

¼ cup mayonnaise

2 tablespoons freshly grated (or prepared) horseradish root

2 tablespoons chopped fresh basil

1 tablespoon freshly squeezed lemon juice

Salt and freshly ground pepper to taste

In a small bowl, mix all ingredients well. Season with salt and pepper. Cover with plastic wrap and refrigerate until ready to serve.

Makes 1 cup

NEW YORK-STYLE CHEESECAKE

COOKIE CRUST

1 cup all-purpose flour

¼ cup sugar

1 teaspoon grated lemon zest

½ teaspoon vanilla extract

1 egg yolk

1 stick (½ cup) unsalted butter, chilled and cut
into ¼-inch pieces

CHEESE FILLING

1½ pounds softened cream cheese

¾ cup granulated sugar

1½ tablespoons all-purpose flour

1½ teaspoons grated lemon zest

1 teaspoon grated orange zest

½ teaspoon pure vanilla extract

3 eggs plus 1 egg yolk

2 tablespoons heavy cream

TO MAKE THE CRUST: Preheat oven to 450°F. Place the flour, sugar, lemon zest, vanilla, egg yolk, and butter in a large mixing bowl. With your fingertips, rub the ingredients together until they are well mixed and can be gathered into a ball. Dust with a little flour, wrap in waxed paper, and refrigerate for at least 1 hour.

Place the chilled dough in an ungreased 9-inch springform pan. With your hands, pat and spread the dough evenly over the bottom and about 2 inches up the side of the pan. Bake in the center of the preheated oven for 10 minutes.

Remove and set aside to cool to room temperature. Lower the oven temperature to 200°F.

TO MAKE THE FILLING: Place the cream cheese in a large mixing bowl and beat vigorously with a wooden spoon until it is creamy and smooth. Beat in the sugar, a few tablespoons at a time, and, when it is well incorporated, beat in the flour, lemon and orange zests, vanilla, eggs and egg yolk, and heavy cream.

Pour the filling into the cooled cookie crust and bake in the center of the oven for 1 hour. Remove from the oven and set aside to cool in the pan. Unmold when cooled and refrigerate the cheesecake for at least 3 hours before serving.

Serves 12

CHERRY CHEESECAKE TOPPING

1 cup grape (or other berry) juice

1 cup dried tart cherries

20 ounces fresh (or frozen) Bing cherries, pitted and halved

½ cup granulated sugar

2 tablespoons brandy

2 teaspoons cornstarch

Bring juice and cherries to a boil in heavy large saucepan. Remove from heat. Cover and let steep for 20 minutes. Bring dried cherry mixture to simmer. Mix in frozen cherries and sugar. Simmer until cherries soften, about 2 minutes for fresh and 5 minutes for frozen.

Mix brandy and cornstarch in bowl to blend. Slowly stir into cherry mixture. Cook over medium heat until mixture boils and thickens, about 1 minute. Cool. Cover with plastic wrap and put in refrigerator to make cold.

Makes 3 cups

Purim

*And Mordechai wrote to all the Jews
that they should make the 14th day of
Adar a day of feasting and gladness, and
of sending portions one to another, and
gifts to the poor.*

THE BOOK OF ESTHER

This holiday is meant to be celebrated with gusto. Jews are quite literally meant to get drunk on this Jewish "Halloween" and go nuts, with God's blessing. Purim marks the time when Haman, a particularly hateful Persian, hatched a plot to kill the Jews. Haman sought to destroy all the Jews that were throughout the whole kingdom of Ahasuerus, even the people of Mordecai.

As told in the Book of Esther, Haman said, "There are a people scattered throughout your land and their laws are diverse from yours...let it be written that they be destroyed." Ahasuerus told Haman, "Do with them as what seems good to you."

His plot failed thanks to the brave Queen Esther, and her courageous uncle, Mordecai; Haman was hanged instead. The *Megillah* (also known as the Book of Esther, a part of the biblical text, the *Mishnah*) tells the story, and is read in the synagogue. Children often dress up as the characters in the story.

I can't remember ever getting loaded on *Purim* as a child, but I do remember being encouraged for the first time to make noise in the sanctuary. Not only were we permitted to be loud, we were given *greggors* (noisemakers) with which to make the noise! Best of all, there were carnival rides in the temple parking lot! Odd for a place where I usually went in my best clothes, hearing endless prompting to stop fidgeting and keep quiet! Dressing up as Esther for the *Purim* parade allowed me a brief chance to feel and act like a queen. Clad in my mother's cast-off costume jewels and wearing a paste tiara, I truly felt the part.

Each time Haman's name is read, children will rattle their *greggors*, to drown out his name. Since the entire Book of Esther must be heard, it can take quite a while to get through the whole story as Haman's name is mentioned more than fifty times

*A person should become so drunk on
Purim that he cannot tell the difference
between "cursed be Haman" and "blessed
be Mordechai."*

BABYLONIAN TALMUD

Jews often observe *Purim* by sending small gifts of
food and drinks to friends and family. Tea, a plate of
hamantaschen (a traditional *Purim* cookie that looks like
a three-cornered hat filled with fruit preserves), or a
box of candy are popular choices. This family recipe
provides instructions for the basic pastry dough.
Many different fillings can be used according to your
personal preference, including apricot, cherry, or
other fruit preserves.

HAMANTASCHEN DOUGH

2½ cups all-purpose flour

2 teaspoons baking powder

1 teaspoon salt

½ cup granulated sugar

¼ cup melted butter

1 medium egg

¾ cup whole milk

Preheat the oven to 375°F. Lightly grease a large cookie sheet. Mix the flour, baking powder, salt, and sugar together in a medium bowl.

Cream the butter and sugar together in a large bowl until smooth. Add the egg and milk. Mix well. Pour the dry ingredients into the large bowl and mix.

Roll the dough out onto a lightly floured surface and cut into rounds, two inches in diameter.

Place one tablespoon of a filling from the recipes below in the middle of the round and draw up three sides to form a triangle. Pinch the corners to seal and bake for about 35 minutes or until lightly browned.

Makes about 24 medium cookies

HAMANTASCHEN ORANGE AND DATE FILLING

1 ¼ cups firmly packed dates, pitted

1 teaspoon grated orange zest

1 ¼ cup orange juice

1 teaspoon ground cinnamon

1 to 2 tablespoons water to thin mixture,
if necessary

In a food processor fitted with a steel blade, pulse all ingredients until it has a smooth pastelike consistency. If the mixture is too sticky to handle, add a tablespoon of water and pulse again. Add an additional tablespoon of water if necessary.

Fills about 24 medium cookies

NOTE: Filling may be made two days ahead and kept in a sealed container in the refrigerator.

HAMANTASCHEN POPPY SEED FILLING

¼ pound poppy seeds

1 egg

¼ cup granulated sugar

Place poppy seeds in a medium heatproof glass bowl and pour boiling water over them. Let stand until the seeds have settled at the bottom of the bowl.

Drain the water and place poppy seeds in a food processor fitted with a steel blade. Pulse a few times, then add egg and sugar and mix thoroughly.

Pour mixture into a medium-sized heavy saucepan and cook over medium heat for about 2 hours or until it becomes very thick. Remove from heat, allow to cool completely.

Fills about 24 medium cookies

NOTE: Filling may be prepared two days ahead and stored in a sealed container in the refrigerator.

TRADITIONAL PRUNE HAMANTASCHEN FILLING

½ pound pitted prunes

2 teaspoons freshly squeezed lemon juice

Grated zest of 1 medium lemon

Soak prunes overnight. Fill medium saucepan with the soaking water and heat prunes over medium heat until soft. Drain well. Place in food processor fitted with a steel blade and pulse until prunes are smooth. Add lemon juice and zest and pulse one or two more times until it is well blended. Filling may be made two days ahead and kept in a sealed container in the refrigerator.

Fills about 24 medium cookies

APPLE-RAISIN
HAMANTASCHEN FILLING

½ cup unsweetened apple butter

¼ cup chopped golden raisins

¼ cup chopped walnuts

I n a bowl, stir together filling ingredients until combined well.

Fills about 24 medium cookies

Sukkot

For in booths did I make the children of Israel dwell when I brought them out of the land of Egypt.

THE TORAH

Sukkot, (booths or temporary huts), is one of the oldest Jewish holidays and may predate even Rosh Hashanah and Yom Kippur. It follows these Days of Awe, falling during a two-week period of Jewish festivals, including *Sukkot, Shemini Atzeret,* and *Simchat Torah.* These holidays are meant to be celebrated in a continuous event.

Sukkot marks two events: the harvesting of the fall crop and a commemoration of the Children of Israel's period of wandering throughout the desert in search of a place to settle after the Exodus. During this time, the Hebrews slept in huts or booths and we build similar structures to live in during the holiday.

The vivid memories I have of *Sukkot* are watching the construction of the *sukkah* in the courtyard of our synagogue, and the strong citrus smell of the *etrog*. Bigger than a lemon but similar, and best gotten when it is still green so that it may ripen in the *sukkah*, the *etrog* is imported from Israel and symbolic of the harvest. Fruits and vegetables hung along the sides of the structure and we ate our snacks within its three walls, singing and reciting prayers of thanksgiving.

> *To everything there is a season and a time to every purpose under heaven.*
> ECCLESIASTES

The *sukkah's* construction must adhere to strict guidelines to be considered an appropriate structure. Builders are told to use leaves or straw as the roof covering and the walls may be made of any material. It must be so well covered that there is more sheltered than open space, but the covering should not be too thick; a heavy rain should penetrate the roof. It must have at least three walls and be beneath the open sky, not under a tree or inside a house. The hut should be decorated with fruits and other harvested food. On the first night of the festival, it is required that at least an olive-sized piece of bread be eaten in the *sukkah*. If meals are eaten, they must be partaken of in the *sukkah*. Sleeping in the *sukkah* is not required in colder climates, thank goodness, since great discomfort nullifies the holiday's requirements of inhabiting the *sukkah* for a full week. Many congregations, particularly ones located in urban settings, build a *sukkah* adjacent to the synagogue for the benefit of congregants who have no *sukkah* of their own, or a place to build one.

Take the fruit of goodly trees, branches of palm trees, and boughs of thick trees, and willows of the brook to rejoice before the Lord.

THE TORAH

HOLISHKES
(STUFFED CABBAGE)

1 pound ground beef

¼ cup uncooked rice

1 egg

1 medium onion, grated

1 medium carrot, peeled and grated

¼ teaspoon salt

12 large green cabbage leaves

¼ cup freshly squeezed lemon juice

½ cup brown sugar

1 cup good-quality tomato sauce

Preheat oven to 350°F. Combine ground beef, rice, and egg in a large bowl. Add onion, carrots, and salt, mix well and set aside. Bring a large kettle of water to boil and blanch cabbage leaves for 2 to 3 minutes. Drain well.

Place a ball of the meat and rice mixture in the middle of one cabbage leaf. Roll up, tucking in ends as you go along so it doesn't fall apart.

Place each rolled leaf in a large frying pan as you finish it, arranging them closely together but with a bit of space between. Add the lemon juice, brown sugar and tomato sauce and then water until all the leaves are covered. Cover tightly and simmer over medium heat for 30 minutes.

Reduce heat to a simmer and cook for another 20 minutes. Remove from flame and bake in oven uncovered for 20 more minutes, turning carefully to brown all over. Add additional water if needed. Serve immediately.

Serves 12 as an appetizer or 6 as a main course

Simchat Torah, Shemini Atzeret, Tu B'shevat, Lag B'omer, and Tisha B'av

These last five holidays are generally overlooked by most Reform Jews. While they are meant to be celebrated, they are somewhat less familiar to all but the most observant. To this day, when my brother and I don't expect something to happen for a while or ever, perhaps we will say, "Yes, it'll happen right around *Tisha B'Av*." I do recall the mention of these holidays in religious school, but I have only a few recollections of their observance.

Sisu V'Simchu B'Simchas Torah
U'snu Kavod La'Torah

TRANSLATION:
Celebrate and rejoice in the joy of the Torah
and give honor to the Torah.
SIMCHAT TORAH TRADITIONAL PRAYER

Simchat Torah is a completely and totally joyful holiday. There is no remembrance of lost Hebrews, fasting, commemorating brave Israelites who died for the right to be Jewish, or even solemnity in the service. It is simply a celebration of the Torah. The yearly reading cycle is started again on this holiday that always falls the day after *Shemini Atzeret*. This post-biblical holiday has no requirements but certain customs have evolved over the years. Some include reading the last section of the last book of the Bible (Deuteronomy) and the first section of the first book (Genesis). The Torahs are all removed from the ark and paraded around the sanctuary by congregants and clergy. Candy is often tossed to the children, as it is on many Jewish holidays.

On *Simchat Torah*, I recall the rabbi removing from the ark one of the many Torahs and taking off the velvet covering with its breathtaking silver adornments. He proceeded to walk through the aisles of the sanctuary and we were permitted to touch the Torah with our prayer books. Though this particular ritual takes places often in most sanctuaries, I think I remember it so well because it was the first time I was old enough to be there and not in children's services.

Shemini Atzeret, the next holiday in this period of festivity, falls on the eighth day of *Sukkot*. In most Reform communities, this holiday is celebrated the same day as *Simchat Torah*. In Orthodox communities, it is observed the following day. The most important aspect of this holiday is a prayer for rain so there will be a fruitful harvest. Some Jewish scholars have argued that saying this prayer and observing the holiday connects us to Israel, because we are praying for rain for a successful harvest there.

TEFILAT GESHEM
(PRAYER FOR RAIN)

Af-Bri is designated as the name of the angel
of rain; to thicken and to form clouds, to empty
them and to cause rain.

Water with which to crown the valley's
vegetation may it not be withheld because of our
unredeemed debt.

In the merit of the faithful Patriarchs protect
the ones who pray for rain.

May He obligate [the Angel Af-Bri] to give us
portions of the segregated rain to soften the
wasteland's face when it
is dry as rock.

With water You symbolized Your might in
Scripture, to soothe with its drops those in
whom was blown a soul, to keep alive the ones
who recall the strengths of the rain.

GOD IS IMPLORED TO PROVIDE HEALTHFUL RAIN TO US IN
THE MERIT OF OUR FOREFATHERS AND OTHER GREAT
LEADERS OF ISRAEL.

DO NOT HOLD WATER BACK! FOR THE SAKE OF HIS
RIGHTEOUSNESS, GRANT ABUNDANT WATER!

REMEMBER THE TWELVE
TRIBES YOU CAUSED
TO CROSS THROUGH THE SPLIT WATERS,
FOR WHOM YOU SWEETENED THE WATER'S BITTER TASTE.
THEIR OFFSPRING WHOSE BLOOD WAS SPILT
FOR YOU LIKE WATER.
TURN TO US—FOR WOES ENGULF OUR SOULS
LIKE WATER.

FOR THE SAKE OF HIS RIGHTEOUSNESS,
GRANT ABUNDANT WATER!

T*u B'Shevat* is a holiday for trees. Before you think "how ridiculous," remember that trees in Israel mean life, and forests mean shade, moisture in a desert, wood for building, and fruit. I remember bringing in money to buy tree certificates for Israel every year of my religious education—there must be a whole Haft forest by now. Though it may seem that this holiday should have gotten its start around the founding of the state of Israel, it is indeed many thousands of years old. During Biblical times, it marked the date after which the harvest was taxed for the next year. Today, observant Jews will eat certain fruits, particularly those from Israel, to mark the holiday.

Lag B'Omer is an abbreviated way of saying "the thirty-third day of the counting of the *omer* (the measure of barley)." Ironically, no one is really sure what this holiday celebrates. It may be an observance of the end of a plague that struck down Talmudic students in biblical times. Traditionally, observant Jews will not plan weddings during the seven weeks between Passover and *Shavuot*, except on *Lag B'Omer*. On this holiday, weddings may be celebrated as they are the rest of the year.

By wisdom is a house built and by understanding it is established.

PROVERBS

The last holiday is *Tisha B'Av* (the ninth day of the month of *Av*). *Tisha B'Av* is regarded by many as the saddest day on the Jewish calendar. It commemorates the destruction of the First and Second Temples in 586 B.C.E. and 70 C.E. The bad luck for Jews on that day didn't end there; Jews were expelled from England in 1290 and from Spain in 1492 on the ninth day of *Av*. During the Holocaust, Nazis with knowledge of the pain this day inflicted on Jews throughout history, made an effort to commit heinous atrocities against them on the same day. It is a day of fasting from the sunset of the night before to the sunset of the following day and observant Jews will sit on the floor as if mourning the death of a loved one. They do not greet one another, much like on Yom Kippur. The only moment of joy found on this day is that some believe that this is the day the Messiah will be born.

> *You shall perform acts of repentance*
> *and to be firm in your faith.*
> *God will not abandon you even*
> *though all seems lost.*
> THE BIBLE

Shalom Aleichem is a hymn chanted on Friday nights upon returning home from the *Shabbat*-eve services, as well as on the eve of festivals and celebrations. This song of peace, introduced in the 17th century, is based on a Talmudic tale of a good angel and an evil angel accompanying every man home from the synagogue on Friday evenings. If they find the house one of love, happiness, and mutual respect, the good angel says, "May the next *Shabbat* be as this one." If the angels find a home of anger, disrespect, and disregard for the Torah, the evil angel says, "May the next *Shabbat* be as this one."

SHALOM ALEICHEM

Shalom aleichem malachay hasharais,
malachay elyon
mimelech malchay hamlachim,
Hakadosh Baruch Hu

Bo'achem l'shalom, malachay hashalom,
malachay elyon
mimelech malchay hamlachim,
Hakadosh Baruch Hu

Barchuni l'shalom, malachay hashalom,
malachay elyon
mimelech malchay hamlachim,
Hakadosh Baruch Hu

Tzeis'chem l'shalom, malachay hashalom,
malachay elyon
mimelech malchay hamlachim,
Hakadosh Baruch Hu

Tzeis'chem l'shalom, malachay hashalom,
malachay elyon
mimelech malchay hamlachim,
Hakadosh Baruch Hu

Translation:
Peace upon you, O ministering angels,
angels of the Exalted One,
from the King Who reigns over the highest
of kings, the Holy One, Blessed is He.

continued...

MAY YOUR COMING BE FOR PEACE, O ANGELS
OF PEACE, ANGELS OF THE EXALTED ONE,
FROM THE KING WHO REIGNS OVER THE HIGHEST
OF KINGS, THE HOLY ONE, BLESSED IS HE.

BLESS ME FOR PEACE, O ANGELS OF PEACE,
ANGELS OF THE EXALTED ONE,
FROM THE KING WHO REIGNS OVER THE HIGHEST
OF KINGS, THE HOLY ONE, BLESSED IS HE.

MAY YOUR DEPARTURE BE FOR PEACE, O ANGELS
OF PEACE, ANGELS OF THE EXALTED ONE,
FROM THE KING WHO REIGNS OVER THE HIGHEST
OF KINGS, THE HOLY ONE, BLESSED IS HE.

Conclusion

To be a good Jew is to know who you are.
You should know how to commemorate those
who died before you so that you can celebrate freely
today, and do your best to assure that future
generations will enjoy the same luxury.

I firmly believe that Judaism is celebrated in the
home and the heart, not in a synagogue on a high
holiday, wearing a new suit and checking out
everyone else's. I love that Judaism and all its
centuries of glorious tradition and perseverance can
take place around a table, with family and friends.

Maybe you don't go to your synagogue's Friday
night services. Try to at least light the candles, roast
a chicken, or even say a quick *bracha* (prayer) over a
glass of Merlot. Buy a *challah* on the way home from
work, and let your kids nosh on it; it makes the best
French toast in the world. Be sure to explain the
basics of the important holidays to your kids so they
don't grow up thinking Chanukah is the Jewish
Christmas and that munching on a snack during Yom
Kippur services is OK. Gather your family together
and rejoice in your "Jewishness;" it must be worth
observing since our religion has lasted as long as it
has against such extraordinary odds.

ADON OLAM

Adon olam, asher malach,
b'terem kol y'tzir nivra.
L'et na'asah v'cheftzo kol,
azai melech sh'mo nikra.
V'acharey kichlot hakol,
l'vado yimloch nora.
V'hu haya, v'hu hoveh,
v'hu yih'yeh b'tifara.
V'hu echad, v'eyn sheni
l'hamshil lo, l'hachbira.
B'li reishit, b'li tachlit,
v'lo ha'oz v'hamisrah.
V'hu Eli, v'chai go'ali,
v'tzur chevli b'et tzarah.
V'hu nisi umanos li,
m'nat kosi b'yom ekra.

B'yado afkid ruchi
b'et ishan v'a'irah.
V'im ruchi g'viyati,
Adonai li v'lo ira.

TRANSLATION:

MASTER OF THE UNIVERSE

THE LORD OF THE UNIVERSE WHO REIGNED

BEFORE ANYTHING WAS CREATED.

WHEN ALL WAS MADE BY HIS WILL

HE WAS ACKNOWLEDGED AS KING.

AND WHEN ALL SHALL END

HE STILL ALL ALONE SHALL REIGN.

HE WAS, HE IS,

AND HE SHALL BE IN GLORY.

AND HE IS ONE, AND THERE IS NO OTHER,

TO COMPARE OR JOIN HIM.

WITHOUT BEGINNING, WITHOUT END

AND TO HIM BELONGS DOMINION AND POWER.

AND HE IS MY GOD, MY LIVING GOD.

TO HIM I FLEE IN TIME OF GRIEF,

AND HE IS MY MIRACLE AND MY REFUGE,

WHO ANSWERS THE DAY I SHALL CALL.

TO HIM I COMMIT MY SPIRIT,

IN THE TIME OF SLEEP AND AWAKENING,

EVEN IF MY SPIRIT LEAVES,

GOD IS WITH ME, I SHALL NOT FEAR.

A Word about Sources

I pulled out the copies of the Torah and the Bible I had been given for my *Bat Mitzvah* and Confirmation and used them as sources for inspiration, quotations, and knowledge about all aspects of Judaism. I also read Rabbi Joseph Telushkin's *Jewish Literacy* and *Jewish Wisdom*, both brilliant works that filled in many blanks for me. The recipes come from two invaluable sources: the index cards my mother has been collecting for decades and a yellowed, brisket-stained, spiral-bound copy of a synagogue cookbook published in 1957 that belonged to my maternal grandmother. The Internet was a valuable resource when searching for the definitive list of the 613 *Mitzvot;* I found the most authoritative version at www.jewfaq.org.

Holiday Recipe List

YOM KIPPUR

Select Yiddish Phrases

Many Jews of a certain age, and sometimes the more observant younger set, will color their language with "Yiddishisms." Yiddish often conveys a feeling or characteristic that English fails to clearly express. Following, find the most popular phrases. A familiarity with any of these expressions will impress even the most reluctant *machetunim*.

ALTER KOCKER: An old man or old woman

BALEBOOSTEH: A compliment to someone who is a terrific housekeeper

BUBBE: Grandmother; an older female who plays an important role in one's life

BUPKES: Nothing; something totally worthless

CHUTZPAH: Brazenness, gall

DRECK: Manure or excrement; inferior merchandise or work; insincere talk or excessive flattery

FRESS: Eat; pig out

GAI GEZUNTERHAIT: Go in good health

GOY: Any person who is not Jewish

KAIN EIN HOREH: No evil eye

KVELL: Glow with pride and happiness, beam; be delighted

KVETCH: Whine, complain; whiner, a complainer

MACHETUNIM: In-laws; the parents of your child's spouse

MAZEL TOV: Good luck; generally used to convey congratulations

MENSCH: A special man or person. One who can be respected

MESHUGGEH: Crazy

NACHES: Joy; gratification, especially from children

NEBBISH: A nobody, simpleton, weakling, awkward person

NOSH: Snack

OY: Exclamation to denote disgust, pain, astonishment, or rapture

SCHLEP: Drag, carry, or haul particularly unnecessary things, parcels, or baggage; to go somewhere unwillingly or where you may be unwanted

SCHMATTA: Rag, anything worthless

SCHNORRER: A beggar who makes pretensions to respectability; sponger, a parasite

SHIKSA: Non-Jewish girl

TCHOTCHKES: Little playthings, ornaments, bric-a-brac, toys

YENTA: Gabby, talkative woman; female blabbermouth

ZAFTIG: Pleasantly plump and pretty; sensuous looking

For wherever you go, I will go;
wherever you lodge, I will lodge;
your people shall be my people,
and your God, my God.

RUTH 1:16

Index